SKILFUL KARATE

Greg McLatchie

A & C Black · London

First published 1990 by
A & C Black (Publishers) Limited
35 Bedford Row, London WC1R 4JH

© 1990 Greg McLatchie

ISBN 0 7136 5779 0

A CIP catalogue record for this book is
available from the British Library.

Cover photograph courtesy of
All Sport Photographic Ltd.

Typeset by Latimer Trend & Company Ltd, Plymouth
Printed and bound in Great Britain by
William Clowes Ltd, Beccles and London.

Right **Performing a left gyaku-tsuki at chudan height**

CONTENTS

ACKNOWLEDGEMENTS

I am grateful to the following people, whose involvement in the book is much appreciated:

Paul Rodgers, department of medical illustration, Hartlepool General Hospital, for providing action photographs

Ken Davis 4th Dan, Colin Ledger 3rd Dan and Joanne Grant 1st Dan of Zanshin Kai, Lenzie; Hamish Adam 5th Dan and Jim Collins 4th Dan of Meadowbank, Edinburgh for modelling in action photographs

Gillian Rodgers and Vera Spaldin for self-defence stills and Cameron McLatchie for demonstrating children's flexibility exercises

Ken Davis and Offox Press for line drawings

Vera Spaldin for typing the manuscript

Hartlepool Health Authority for use of hospital facilities.

'Seiza': students mirror the movements of their instructor before the training session begins

INTRODUCTION

Karate is a popular and enjoyable sport which fosters both physical fitness and life-saving skills. It is relatively cheap to learn and has the added advantage that it can be practised throughout life from childhood to old age. The grading system permits continuous improvement and matching of equivalent abilities in competition.

This book has three aims. Firstly, it is a guide to karate from basic technique to competition and 1st Dan black belt level. Illustrations are in simple three or four stage manoeuvres.

Secondly, self-defence situations are presented with the emphasis being laid on thwarting an attack in the simplest manner and 'buying time' to get away. The legal implications of possessing karate skills are also discussed.

Thirdly, there are sections on the prevention and management of injury. Your training will be more regular and successful if you can learn to recognise risk situations and take avoiding action. Warm-up and flexibility exercises are described as well as the correct action to take when someone is injured.

Throughout the book coaches and karateka are, in the main, referred to individually as 'he'. This should, of course, be taken to mean 'he or she' where appropriate.

A young woman initiates her defence against an attempted assault from behind

KARATE

Karate means 'empty hand'. In its simplest sense the word is applied to the sport of karate and empty-handed combat without the assistance of weapons. In the deepest sense it implies self-discipline, religious conviction and a wealth of knowledge, patience and understanding.

a method *par excellence* of developing fitness. Although it had been practised as a sport in Japanese universities, its popularity mushroomed in the West. By the early 1970s, following films such as *Enter the Dragon* starring Bruce Lee, it was estimated that 60,000–100,000 people in the United Kingdom had taken up the sport.

History and development

The origins of karate can be traced to China, but the modern form is said to owe its development to the Okinawan islanders who, when overrun in the early seventeenth century by oppressors who banned the use of weapons of any kind, developed a system of unarmed combat which proved most effective. Trained exponents of their method were able to dismount horsemen with jumping kicks and then punch through their bamboo armour with their hardened fists. As the discipline developed, weaponry such as the rice-flail was ingeniously introduced.

In 1917 karate was introduced to the Japanese mainland, where its development continued with the formation of five main styles: Shotokan, Shitoryu, Gojuryu, Wadoryu and Shukokai. Since then numerous sub-developments have taken place, all of which have their roots in the classic teachings.

After the Second World War, General MacArthur (commander of US forces in the Far East) endorsed the development of karate by encouraging its instruction to American servicemen. In this way karate was transported to the Western world, where it developed not only as an effective form of self-defence but as

Forces in karate

The peak velocity attained by a straight punch executed by a trained exponent is 35–40 m.p.h. (56–64 k.p.h.) with a force exerted of 3,000 Newtons or 675lbs per square inch. These figures are proportionally higher for kicks. A velocity of 20 m.p.h. (32 k.p.h.) is sufficient to break a 2in-thick (5cm) block of wood and one of around 30 m.p.h. (48 k.p.h.) is sufficient to break concrete. The secret of the karate blow is the concentration of this energy in a small striking surface area, for example the first and second knuckles only.

All karate exponents (*karateka*) are aware that wood is easier to break than concrete. The reason for this is that only part of the energy is actually transferred to the target; the remainder is transferred to the striking fist, where it is experienced as pain. Although wood will absorb most of the hand's kinetic energy, concrete obstinately refuses at least half of it. This presents a psychological problem to even the most hardened of karateka.

A further mystery is why the bones of the hand do not break when striking wood or concrete. This is because bone is much tougher than either, and provided the forces are directed along the lines of stress in the bone, no damage will be sustained. Implicit in this is the posture of the striking hand or foot which must be correct if injury is to be prevented. Remember this in all aspects of karate training and practice.

Competition karate

This is a regular feature of modern karate which is increasing in popularity. Once exclusive to men, it now attracts women and children. Weight and grading categories have permitted a wide range of participation so that many exponents have the opportunity to become winners. Most competitions are of three types: traditional, semi-contact and full-contact.

Traditional competition

This remains the most popular form of competition. Contests last two to three minutes. Blows are directed at specific targets on an opponent but are withdrawn just before or at contact. Points are scored on the basis of half points (*waza-ari*) or full points (*ippon*) depending on the style, quality and intensity of the technique. As bodily contact should be light or non-existent, difficulties occasionally arise in the scoring of competitions. Therefore, anatomical drawings are shown on page 82 to assist decision making and awareness of vulnerable areas of the human body.

Semi-contact competition

In some styles (e.g. Kyokushinkai) the rules permit full contact to the body with punches and kicks. High kicks to the side of the head and sweeps or kicks to the legs are also allowed. A full point and subsequently a win is given for a good knockdown or a knockout, which is said to have occurred if the fighter is unable to stand up within five seconds of being knocked down. Half a point is given if the technique floors a fighter who is nevertheless able to get up again within five seconds. After each round competitors are required to demonstrate their ability at woodbreaking (*tameshiwari*) before progressing to the next one. The weapons (in order of use) are the straight punch, the side of the hand and the elbow. Each contest lasts two to three minutes.

Full-contact competition

This is a more recent development which bears many resemblances to Thai boxing. Blows of unrestrained velocity are directed with the hands or feet against the opponent. The contest is fought in rounds as in boxing, and the winner is the fighter who accumulates most points or who succeeds in knocking out his opponent.

Kata

Kata are prearranged forms or contests against imaginary opponent(s). They are conducted with rhythm and commitment and are valuable in developing concentration and good technique. They are also a specific feature of competition karate which have developed a strong following.

KARATE FOR SPORT AND SELF-DEFENCE

Karate is a martial art (Mars=Roman god of war). It originated as a method of self-defence and effective counterattack, then developed into a sport. It is almost unique as an activity in that, as well as being a method of achieving overall physical fitness, its techniques can also be used to save lives. The recent increase in urban violence has doubtless contributed to its growing popularity.

Who can practise?

Men, women and children can benefit from practising karate. Provided that there are no physical disabilities, age is no bar in adults. An ideal starting age for children is around 8 years old.

Getting started

The ideal way to learn is to join a reputable club with well-qualified instructors. Most of these are recognised by the Sports Council, and you should inquire at your local sports centre.

Before joining, prospective karateka should watch one or two classes to get the 'feel' of the sport. Most instructors welcome and encourage this. At this time, questions of cost of practising at the club and the type of equipment required can also be answered.

Karate suits can usually be bought at the club itself or at martial arts shops. Costs vary, but discounts are usually given to club members. The ideal is eventually to have two (or even three) suits so that one is always clean. If only one suit is available it should be washed as regularly as possible – at least twice a week – and allowed to dry overnight before being neatly ironed. Fresh kit is vitally important in maintaining personal hygiene and preventing infection (especially fungal).

As karate is conducted barefoot, adequate footcare is essential. A pair of zori sandals or flip-flops should be worn from the changing room to the dojo itself. They are not permitted on the dojo floor and should be left neatly at the side. The feet should be quickly washed in warm water after each training session, then dried and exposed for several minutes before the socks are put on. Special attention should be paid to drying between the toes.

Protective equipment

Although not vital for beginners, it is advisable to acquire the following as expertise increases: gumshield, groin guard (men/boys) and padded or sports brassière (women/girls). There are various types of protective padding which are permitted during competition and sparring. These can usually be acquired from instructors or martial arts shops.

Dojo etiquette

It is important to realise that a standard form of behaviour is recognised and expected in traditional karate. When the class begins, the students stand facing the instructor (sensei=master) and then mirror his movements.

At the command of 'Yoi' the hands are brought to the sides of the body and the feet come together. At the command 'Seiza' the sensei adopts the full squat position, then the left knee is placed on the floor, followed by the right knee (reflecting the ancient Japanese method of sword-drawing). The left hand is placed on the floor followed by the right, thumbs and indices touching. The sensei nods to the most senior student who commands 'Sensei ni rei'; the students then bow, giving the salutation, 'Oss'. When the sensei stands up, it is the most senior student on his extreme left who rises first, followed by the next most senior on his immediate left and so on.

At the end of the class the command 'Seiza' is given; the above procedure is observed, followed by the command 'Mokso' in which the hands are clasped, the eyes are closed and rhythmic breathing is observed during a period of meditation. After this the sensei rises and nods to the most senior student, who gives the command 'Sensei ni rei' at which the class bow and utter 'Oss'.

On entering and leaving the dojo it is customary to bow and say 'Oss'.

The grading system

Karate observes a formal grading system which indicates the level of expertise reached by students and gives automatic recognition of seniority. Although there are variations, most styles award coloured belts for each grade as shown in the following table.

Grade	Belt
9th kyu (student)	white (some styles award red)
8th kyu	orange
7th kyu	yellow
6th kyu	green
5th kyu	purple (occasionally blue)
4th kyu	purple with a white band (occasionally purple)
3rd kyu	brown
2nd kyu	brown (sometimes brown with a white band)
1st kyu	brown with a white band (sometimes brown with a red band)
1st Dan (step)	black

PREPARATION AND TRAINING

The essentials for success in karate are flexibility; stamina; power; practice and a positive mental attitude leading to good technique.

Flexibility

This aspect of training should not be neglected. Increased flexibility can only be acquired with practice. It increases your chances of developing good technique, improves your scoring repertoire in competition and prevents injury. Exercises should be performed daily, morning and evening if possible, and certainly always before the karateka starts to train. Little energy is required, and many of the movements performed stretch the muscle groups used in karate and prime them ready for action.

In most karate classes two types of exercise are performed.

Ballistic exercises

These involve bobbing or bouncing up and down to stretch the required muscle group, sometimes with a partner. Although increased mobility is acquired, there is little control of the range over which the muscle has been stretched.

Static exercises

These are controlled stretching movements. The muscle group is stretched until tightness is felt, and the position is held for several seconds. The muscles are then relaxed and the movements are repeated. As the muscles warm up, the range of movement is increased. There is less risk of injury in static stretching than in ballistic exercises.

In practice, combinations of ballistic and static exercise are used. Both can be performed with a partner, who should always be someone trustworthy.

Examples

Neck exercise

Start by gently moving your head from side to side, then backwards and forwards. Look over each shoulder alternately. At the limit of the movement the muscles of your neck should feel tight and the position should be held for a count of five or ten.

Shoulder exercise

Raise your arms in the air, gently rotating them through the full range of shoulder movements.

Trunk exercise

Carry out rotational movements from side to side, then slide the fingers of one hand down the leg of the same side, stretching over the head with the other arm.

Hip exercise

Rotate the hips.

When leaning to the side, make sure that you don't bend forwards from the waist

Knees are rotated while keeping the legs bent

Knee and ankle exercise

Place your hands on your bent knees. Keep the heel flat on the floor. When your Achilles tendons feel tight, do not squat any further. Gently rotate from this position.

Adductor muscles/Achilles tendon exercise

Adopt the squat position. Gently but firmly push the knees backwards whilst pressing down the buttocks so that the adductor muscles feel tight. Increase the tension by moving slowly from side to side.

Stretching the adductor muscles and Achilles tendons

Combined hamstring/adductor/Achilles tendon stretch

From the position shown increase the tension on your muscles by turning away and by bending forwards.

Full hamstring stretch

Sit down with your legs together; bend forwards from the waist, trying to get your chin on to your shins (or until the muscles at the back of your legs feel tight). Hold the position for a count of 5–10 and repeat.

Splits

As flexibility increases, attempt to get as low as possible in side to side splits (adductor stretch) and fore and aft splits (hamstring and quadriceps stretch of alternate legs).

The right leg should be at right angles to the left leg

Make sure that you bend from the waist and keep your back as flat as possible. Don't try to push your head forwards out of alignment with your back to get nearer to the floor!

Stretching with a partner

Ask your partner to elevate the limb being stretched until tightness can be felt. Hold the position for a count of 10. Relax and repeat.

Stretching exercises with children

Emphasise the importance of careful stretching to avoid injury. Children are usually very good at following advice, provided it is thoughtfully given, and can usually achieve a high level of flexibility (which is often present from the outset). Make sure you do not overstretch young muscles.

Stamina

Stamina or endurance is best acquired by circuit training exercises and road running. These should be incorporated into your training programme as they increase fitness and allow a variety of training which is important in preventing staleness.

The type of circuit training can be varied and one method is to carry out short bursts of exercise for three to four minutes at a time with 30–60 seconds' rest between exercises. The boxing rounds system of 6–8 three-minute rounds with 30 seconds' rest between works very well. In the example shown below there are skill, flexibility and some strengthening exercises. Intensive stamina training should not be started without an introductory period of three to four weeks of running, cycling or swimming covering gradually increasing distances.

Example schedule

	Exercise	Time	Rest period
1.	Sit ups	3 minutes	30 seconds
2.	Skipping	3 minutes	30 seconds
3.	Squat jumps	3 minutes	30 seconds
4.	Punching the heavy bag	3 minutes	30 seconds
5.	Kicking the heavy bag	3 minutes	30 seconds
6.	Skipping	3 minutes	30 seconds

Your partner can help this stretching exercise by pressing gently down above the kneecap of the raised leg

Ensure that children are given proper instruction in all warming-up exercises

15

Such a 'rounds' schedule can be varied considerably. If you feel on good form it can be preceded by a short fast run (one to three miles or kilometres). If you wish, you can also introduce some lightweight high repetition weight exercises.

Running

Running is an exercise used in the training of most sportsmen and women to increase stamina, and many karateka make use of running as part of their training schedule. The aim should be to vary your running as much as possible, covering enough distance to ensure an increase in fitness but interspersing it with short sharp sprints to maintain speed and power. Running should be carried out on a regular basis, for example, three to four times a week, covering one to five miles (or kilometres) depending on form.

Power

Power is acquired by using high resistance and low repetition exercises such as weight-lifting or working on a multi-gym. Such exercises increase both bulk and power. Make sure that the exercises are correctly demonstrated and that you perform them as instructed.

Example programme 1

Approximately 10 repetitions per exercise

Cycle 1

1. Legs – Bench step up with weight
2. Biceps – Barbell curl
3. Triceps – Parallel bar dips with weight
4. Abdomen – Crunches (middle and upper abdominals)
5. Back – Lateral machine pull down behind back
6. Shoulders – Upright rowing
7. Chest – Bench press

Cycle 2

1. Legs – Leg press
2. Biceps – Alternate biceps curl
3. Triceps – Rear bench dips
4. Abdominal – Incline twisting sit ups
5. Back – Bent arm barbell pull over
6. Shoulders – Alternate dumb-bell press
7. Chest – Incline press

Cycle 3

1. Legs – Squats
2. Biceps – Incline curl
3. Triceps – Lat machine close grip pull down
4. Abdominal – Hanging leg raise (lower abs)
5. Back – Dead lift
6. Shoulders – Press behind neck
7. Chest – Flying

Start cycle 1 by going from the first exercise through to the seventh as quickly as you can and without stopping between each exercise. On finishing this first set of exercises you are allowed a short rest (two minutes). Try to cut this down to one minute as you get fitter. After this short rest you should repeat the same cycle between three and five times, depending on your fitness. If after a while you start to find this easy you may add cycle 2 and then cycle 3. These should follow the same system as cycle 1: approximately seven exercises, one per body part. With this method you should increase muscle strength and, even more important for the contest karateka, stamina and speed. As your schedule gets easier, add more weight, a little at a time, rather than more repetitions. Your schedule should be carried out at least three days per week, every day if you have time. A typical range of weightlifting exercises and schedules are also included with suggested starting poundages. You, however, are the judge of your own ability and must experiment with your schedule and training poundages.

Example programme 2

1. Snatches from the 'hang'

Stand with insteps under the bar and the feet about shoulder-width apart. Use an overhand grip on the bar with the hands at a distance of elbow to elbow apart. Stand erect and let the bar hang at thigh level. From this position, in a single movement pull on the bar until it is overhead. Lower and repeat. You will have to bend slightly forwards in order to get momentum to accelerate the movement of the bar upwards.

2. Upright rowing

Use a narrow overhand grip, with hands about 6in (15cm) apart. Stand erect, let the bar hang and pull upwards in front of the chest to the root of the neck. Lower and repeat.

3. Back and forward press

Use an overhand grip, with the hands shoulder-width apart. Lift the bar from the floor to the chest. Press the bar upwards, lower the bar behind the neck, press the bar upwards and lower to the chest. Repeat the exercise.

4. Alternate dumb-bell press

Lift dumb-bells to shoulder level and press them alternately above the head.

5. Two-hands barbell curl

Use an underhand grip with the hands shoulder-width apart, letting the bar hang at arm's length. With both arms parallel to the body and using biceps only, curl the bell until it lies across the root of the neck. Lower and repeat.

6. French press

Use an overhand grip on the barbell with the hands about 8–12in (20–30cm) apart. Raise the bar directly overhead and then gently lower it, bending the elbows only so that it goes behind

the head. Straighten the arms and repeat. This is an excellent triceps exercise.

7. Zottman curl

Using dumb-bells, alternatively curl the weight with each hand. When the weight is curled the hands should rotate as the dumb-bell is gradually lowered again.

8. Reverse press-ups

Place your feet on a bench, with the hands on another bench, and lower your body between the two. This is another excellent triceps exercise.

9. Squat clean from the hang

It is better to learn this exercise in the first instance, but a simple variation is front squats. Using an overhand grip, raise the bar to the shoulders and, holding it in that position, squat downwards. Raise and repeat the exercise.

10. Heel raises

With the bar raised behind the neck, lift yourself up and on to tiptoe before lowering yourself again.

11. Bench press

Lie flat on the bench with hands elbow to elbow apart. Press the bar from the chest to arm's length. Lower and repeat.

12. Bent arm pullover

Lying on the bench, using an overhand grip with hands about 12in (30cm) apart, lower the bar over your head until it almost touches the floor when you have your arms bent. Then pull the bar over your head until it reaches the base of your neck and repeat the manoeuvre.

13. Alternate sit ups on the incline

Use the incline bench. Keep your legs bent. Do sit-ups, alternately twisting to the right and to the left.

14. Leg raises on the incline

Again with the incline bench, raise your legs until you feel your abdominal muscles tighten. Lower and repeat.

15. Dumb-bell side bend

With one dumb-bell, bend as far sidewards as is possible and straighten up again. Repeat this each side.

possible. Do up to a hundred repetitions if possible, provided that you do them in rapid style.

For the first fortnight do one set of each exercise and then add another set. Always strive to increase speed and stamina. Drink only enough to quench thirst. After two months' training has been completed, if training enthusiasm is at a high peak, add a third set. Get plenty of sleep – eight hours at least. If you become stale, stop training for one week then resume at one set each and work up in the usual manner. On off-nights reduce repetitions and shorten distance of roadwork. On a good night push yourself to the limit. Run every night or every day if possible, but restrict longer runs to twice weekly. Short runs can be done in lighter clothing.

Programme 2 (Super set: **after performing the first exercise, carry on to the next without resting**)

Suggested/starting poundages		Sets	No. of repetitions
45–55	1 Warm-up snatches from the hang	1 or 2	10–20
40–50	2 Upright rowing	SS* 2 or 3	12–20
40–50	3 Back and forward press		
15–20	4 Alternate dumb-bell press	3	12
50	5 Two-hands barbell curl	SS* 2 or 3	10–15
50	6 French press		
15–20	7 Zottman curl	SS* 2 or 3	15–20
Nil	8 Reverse press-ups		
75	9 Squat clean from the hang	SS*	15–35
150–200	10 Heel raises		40
75–100	11 Bench press		
50	12 Bent arm pullover	SS* 3	15–20
Nil	13 Alternate situps on incline	SS* 3	max.
Nil	14 Leg raises on incline		
30	15 Dumb-bell side bend	2 each	up to 60

SS* – super sets

When possible, at least twice a week, you should aim to do roadwork for about one hour in warm clothing, that is tracksuit, hood, towel, T-shirt, gloves and boots. Jog, trot and sprint, run backwards, high knee raising and so on.

Allow yourself three workouts to find the most suitable training poundages for your own requirements, then keep to it.

Use light weights and work fast with minimum rest between sets. When exercise becomes easier increase repetitions, not poundages, and work up to very high reps if

Practice and positive mental attitude

The first attempts at performing new techniques usually appear unco-ordinated. However, the movements are not unnatural and, with constant practice, they become almost automatic. Practise the movements taught to you by your instructor in class as he commands, then practise all newly learned movements at home, on a daily basis if possible. The ideal times are usually first thing in the morning and in the evening.

Carry out all practice with determination and spirit ('ki'). Develop a positive approach to your training, learn your basics well and acquire the necessary fitness and flexibility to enjoy your sport.

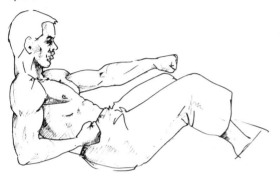

With knees bent, and back raised from the floor, punching alternately with the left and the right fist is an excellent exercise for developing stamina and abdominal strength

How to assess your fitness

As your training proceeds it is encouraging to know either that your fitness is increasing or that you have maintained an already high level of fitness. The training schedules described will bring about an increase in cardiovascular fitness (heart and lung fitness), which allows more oxygen to be supplied to the muscle cells of the body. Increase in cardiovascular fitness is based on the so-called loading principle. You must first apply a load to the oxygen supply system (the heart and lungs) which is slightly greater than it can easily cope with. The body adapts to this load so that it becomes easier, indicating an increase in fitness; this is the basis of the circuit training.

Pulse counting

How much stress you can place on yourself can be assessed by the technique of pulse counting. Count your pulse at the wrist for one minute. This is the Resting Pulse Rate (RPR). The Loading Pulse Rate (LPR) is the increase that you must achieve to improve the oxygen supply system to your muscles. It can be calculated from the following formula:

$$\text{necessary increase required} = \frac{3}{5} \times \left(220 - \frac{\text{your age}}{\text{(years)}} - RPR\right).$$

For example, if you are 25 years old with an RPR of 60 beats per minute you have to increase your pulse by:

$$\frac{3}{5} \times (220 - 25 - 60) = 3 \times \frac{135}{5}$$
$$= 3 \times 27 = 91 \text{ beats per minute.}$$

You must, therefore, aim for a pulse rate increase of 91 beats per minute to be maintained for at least 15 minutes per session. This increase plus your RPR is the Loading Pulse Rate, that is 151 beats per minute.

If you apply this principle you only need a stop-watch in the dojo to measure and improve your fitness.

Pertinent factors about warm-up

Flexibility exercises performed for taking part in karate training are usually followed initially by some light exercises before training proper is undertaken. This is a warm-up period which is important for the following reasons.

1. Warm-up increases the speed and force of muscle contraction.
2. Warm-up related to a particular activity improves muscle 'memory' and therefore co-ordination.
3. Warm-up prevents injury to muscles, tendons and ligaments.
4. Warm-up brings on the second 'wind' more rapidly.

Guidelines for warming up properly

1. The warm-up should be strenuous enough to increase body temperature and cause light perspiration, but should not lead to tiredness.
2. It should include stretching and loosening exercises.

3. It should include movements common to the sport to be undertaken.
4. It should not be exhausting.
5. It should begin 10–15 minutes before taking part in the exercise proper.
6. Keep warm during warm-up and afterwards by remaining active.
7. At the end of the training session carry out light exercises as part of your warm-down before showering and changing.

The training diet

Energy for muscular activity comes from dietary intake. Much of this is provided by a complex carbohydrate called glycogen. It is present in muscle and is stored in the liver. Glycogen is broken down as energy is required. Since glycogen is so vital for performance, ensuring an adequate store is the most likely way that your performance can be improved.

Basic dietary requirements

Like other people the karateka requires at least normal amounts of proteins, carbohydrates and fats. The daily diet should include four parts carbohydrate to one part of protein and fat. This is because much of our energy comes from using carbohydrates and the daily requirement for protein is not as high as was once believed.

Thus the three main foods are protein, carbohydrates and fat. In addition, vitamins, minerals and water are necessary.

Protein

Proteins are especially preponderant in eggs, lean meat, milk and cheese in the form of animal protein; or wheat and rye and green vegetables in the form of vegetable protein. They are not an important source of energy and only become so during starvation. One may think that eating a high protein diet would automatically increase muscle size. However, this is not the case, as protein is excreted if it exceeds 15–20 per cent of the dietary intake, so under normal training circumstances it is unnecessary.

Fats

Fats are the energy storehouse of the body. They also provide a source of muscle energy under exercise conditions. Generally speaking, during light exercise we rely on carbohydrate for muscular energy but, as we work harder, fats become important. During exhaustive work muscle energy comes from a combination of carbohydrate and fat. Fats are available in animal or vegetable form from foods such as fish, butter, milk or cream.

Carbohydrates

Carbohydrates are sugars and starches. They should make up at least 50 per cent of the total calorific intake. The principal sugar is glucose. Only a little of this is stored in the body, in the liver. During exhaustive exercise, if no additional carbohydrates were taken we would use up the store of energy in two hours. You might have heard of the process of 'glycogen loading' or 'carbohydrate loading'. Chronic muscular exhaustion can result from an extremely strenuous regime of training. Studies have shown that this is related to depletion of the carbohydrate complex already mentioned which is present in muscle, called glycogen. In very active muscles it supplies their energy but after 2–3 days of exercise, such as long distance runs of greater than 10–15 miles (16–24km) per day, it will be reduced to near zero. It has been shown that even a high carbohydrate intake will not replace this quickly, despite rest. Therefore, to achieve excellence in performance, distance runners eat only protein or fats in their diet for several days during heavy training. This allows the depletion of muscle glycogen, then they start a very high carbohydrate diet for three to four days to coincide with the race. This is said to improve performance and delay exhaustion. Repeated carbohydrate loading may not be effective for repeated races. It is unlikely to be of benefit in karate but may assist you if part of your training involves long runs.

How many meals?

We have limited ability to store readily available carbohydrate energy. This is dependent on a regular intake of food energy. During training you should eat at 4–6 hourly intervals throughout the day. The single evening meal and intermittent snacks during the day will not provide the best training basis. Each meal should include adequate carbohydrates.

Are extra vitamins necessary?

On theoretical grounds it has been felt that additional Vitamin E might increase performance. However, all experimental work on athletes to date has failed to record an improved performance with this vitamin.

Similarly Vitamin C, in large quantities, has failed to improve performance but there is some evidence that it may protect against viral illnesses such as the common cold. For this reason Vitamin C supplements may be of value.

The Vitamin B group, that is thiamine, riboflavin and nicotinic acid, are all involved in carbohydrate metabolism. Again, provided that adequate amounts are being taken no deficiency will arise. The recommended intake for each 1,000 calories is thiamine: 0.4mg; riboflavin: 0.44mg; and nicotinic acid: 6.6mg. Further increases will simply be excreted.

Glucose drinks

From studies of cyclists, evidence has shown that glucose-containing drinks will cause an increase in blood sugar even during severe exercise. Concurrent with this is improved performance. These drinks may provide extra energy for a full day's competition.

Recovery from exhaustion

Glucose syrup taken after exhausting exercise speeds recovery. So, after longer runs of five miles and more, drink containing glucose should be taken in addition to your normal diet. This will also help you to train more efficiently the following day.

Anabolic steroids

Although widely used, these drugs remain illegal in Britain today. They have many potential side effects varying from acne and tiredness to diabetes and liver cancer. However, there is little doubt that they increase muscle mass, recovery time between training sessions and even aggression.

The problem with these drugs is that they are often taken without medical control and, unless there is a change of philosophy, this will continue to be the case. Therefore it is in your best interests to stay clear of steroids when training, both for health reasons and because of the likelihood of disqualification if you are discovered.

Finally, it is necessary to be aware of the danger of anabolic steroids for the child athlete. This can lead to premature fusion of the growing ends of bones and to stunted height.

THE NATURAL WEAPONS OF KARATE

Karate makes remarkable use of our available physical attributes, in particular the hand and the arm, and the foot and the leg.

Hand and arm

Making a fist

Hand injuries can be prevented by ensuring correct punching techniques. It is therefore important to know how to make a fist properly. The striking surface of the fist should be with the knuckles of the index and middle fingers because they are immobile and the force of the blow passes directly to the solid arm bone – the radius. To make a fist, curl the fingers tightly into the palm and press the thumb over them.

Then turn the wrist slightly so that the first two knuckles make a straight line with the radial bone of the forearm.

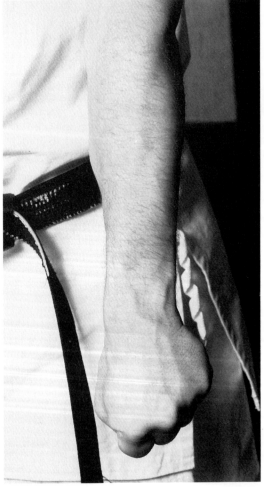

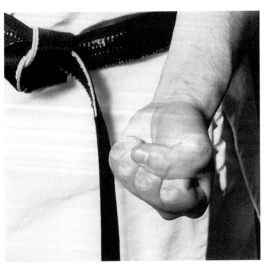

Example of a correct fist, with thumb pressed over fingers

The first two knuckles are in line with the radial bone of the forearm

The following are some variations of a normal fist (seiken).

Uraken – back fist

The knuckles of the index and ring finger are used to strike the opponent's face and head (see 'Basic techniques').

Kentsui – hammer fist

In this technique the muscular border of the clenched fist is used to strike downwards (like a hammer). The target is the opponent's head or neck.

Shuto uchi (synonym = tegatana) – hand sword

In this technique the fleshy edge of the open hand is used to strike the opponent's neck or clavicles (collar bones). The technique has gained notoriety as a famous karate chop, although it is rarely used in any form of competition karate.

Nukite – piercing fingers

The fingers are used as the striking surface to the opponent's abdomen or face. They can be used singly or as a combination. Although this technique is well described in karate, it is not used in competition and lends itself easily to dislocation of the fingers if incorrectly carried out.

Haito

This variation of hand technique uses the inside (thumb) edge of the hand to strike the opponent's neck.

Nukite – if all fingers are used in a striking technique, the second and third can be bent slightly to align with the first to avoid injury on impact

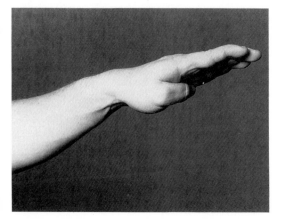

Left **Haito – the thumb must be kept on the palm to avoid dislocation**

Empi – the elbow

The elbow can be used as a weapon to strike upwards in uppercut fashion, or downwards, backwards or sideways.

Foot and leg

The leg is much more powerful than the arm, so kicks can generate much greater velocity than punches. During kicking techniques it is important to maintain balance and to be able to execute the kick as quickly as possible. A slow or telegraphed technique lends itself easily to counterattack, the opponent grabbing the kicking foot and either sweeping the attacker off balance or countering with a punch.

Naka-ashi – the ball of the foot

For the ball of the foot to be used effectively as a striking surface the toes must be firmly pulled upwards as shown. The most common technique for which the ball of the foot is used is *mae-geri* (front kick) and *mawashi geri* (roundhouse kick).

The toes are pulled well back when kicking with the ball of the foot

Seashi – the instep

The instep is used as a striking surface for both mae-geri and mawashi geri (see 'Basic techniques').

Kakato – the heel

The heel can be used as an offensive weapon in stamping after the opponent has been swept to the ground. It is also used as a striking surface for *ushiro-geri* (back kick), the target being the face, chest or abdomen of the opponent.

Ashigatana – side of the foot (foot sword)

The outer, fleshy edge of the foot is commonly used as a striking surface in *yoko-geri* (side kick). The targets of attack are the face, neck, abdomen or joints, usually the hip and knee.

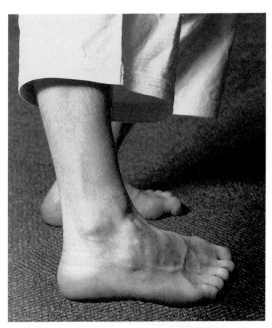

The side of the foot can be used in a foot strike

Hiza – the knee

Use of the knee in karate is analogous to the use of the elbow. It can be used to deliver powerful blows, especially when fighting close to the opponent. The targets of attack from a knee thrust are the face of a held opponent, the abdomen or the groin. The thrust can also be used in knockdown styles of karate to strike the thigh and so weaken the opponent.

KARATE STANCES

Many of the foot positions in karate have been copied from the aggressive or defensive postures adopted by animals and birds during flight or flight situations. Of the variations which you will learn some are extremely common.

Zenkutsu-dachi (the forward stance or inclined posture)

This is one of the most commonly adopted stances in karate and is a useful base for initiating either kicking or punching techniques. The fighter in this stance can move forwards or backwards with equal ease. The ideal position of the feet will vary according to height but they are generally about 2ft 6in (76cm) apart. The advanced leg is bent so that from knee to heel the lower leg is almost perpendicular to the ground. The rear leg is extended.

Kokutsu-dachi (back stance)

This is a defensive posture and is usually combined with a blocking technique. From the blocking position a counterattack with a punch can easily be executed.

Zenkutsu-dachi – the height of this stance depends on the style of karate being practised

Kokutsu-dachi – 70% of the karateka's weight is on his back leg and 30% is on his front leg

Neko-ashi-dachi (the cat stance)

Although this is mainly a stance used in karate kata, it is a useful stance from which to execute a front kick and is occasionally used for this purpose in competitions.

Kiba-dachi (the equestrian stance)

In this stance the legs and feet are parallel, and the knees are bent. The posture is similar to that of riding a horse with the feet in the stirrups.

Shiko-dachi (the sumo posture)

This stance has been derived from sumo wrestling, and because of its relative immobility is rarely used in competition techniques, although it does appear in karate kata. The feet are planted with toes pointing inwards and spread to about twice the shoulder breadth. The knees are then bent, the back being kept straight. The posture itself is useful for building thigh strength.

Sochin-dachi (the fighting stance)

In this posture, which is similar to zenkutsu-dachi, the legs are slightly wider apart, the body weight distributed equally between both feet, the toes of which point in the same direction. Both knees are also slightly bent.

Heiko-dachi (the parallel stance)

The feet are placed less than a shoulder-width apart and are parallel for all of their length.

Neko-ashi-dachi or cat stance

Sochin-dachi – the karateka's weight is distributed evenly between both legs

DEFENCE TECHNIQUES (UKE)

Blocks (*uke*) are of three types – upper, middle and lower – and are executed against attacks from punches or kicks.

Upper blocks

Age-uke (the rising block)

Position 1

Stand in heiko-dachi (the parallel stance), with the fists in the ready position.

Position 2

For a left-handed rising block, extend the right arm upwards, bringing the left blocking arm round the body.

Position 3 – the completed block

This block is executed in defence against attacks to the face and head.

Middle blocks

Chudan-soto-uke (outside middle block) and chudan-uchi-uke (inside middle block)

These blocks are executed against attacks to the abdomen and chest.

Finishing position for age-uke. The forearm slopes so that a descending strike would be deflected

Chudan-uchi-uke

Position 1

From the heiko-dachi position extend the left arm forwards, bringing the right arm round the trunk. Then sharply withdraw the left arm and fist backwards while rotating the right arm outwards to block the oncoming attack.

The right fist should be no higher than the right shoulder

Chudan-soto-uke

Position 1

Stand in heiko-dachi.

First movement for chudan-soto-uke. The left arm should be pushed out straight at shoulder height. The exact distance from the hip of the right arm depends on the karate style being practised

Position 2

With the left arm extended, raise the right arm to head level.

First movement for chudan-soto-uke

Position 3

Complete the block by bringing the right arm sharply downwards while simultaneously withdrawing the left arm and fist to belt level.

The block is completed in front of the body. The arm does not need to cross over the body very much – it just has to deflect slightly to one side a strike aimed at the stomach

Lower block

Gedan-barai (lower block)

Position 1

Stand in heiko-dachi.

Position 2

Extend the right arm towards the midline, and raise the left arm and fist to head level.

Position 3

Complete the block by bringing the left arm sharply downwards to ward off the attack and simultaneously and sharply withdraw the right clenched fist backwards to belt level.

Practical demonstrations of the use of blocks

Example 1

Position 2 for gedan-barai. Make sure that the left fist does not rest on the right shoulder and that the right arm is pushed out

Attack to the mid-body. The attacker attempts a right-handed oi-tsuki (lunge punge) which is effectively blocked by a chudan-uchi-uke

The aborted attack is then countered with an elbow strike to the side of the head

Example 2

The attacker attempts a right front kick which is blocked by gedan-barai

Successful defence is then followed up with a left gyaku-tsuki to the side of the head

Basic techniques

Mastery of the basic techniques is fundamental to expertise in karate. They comprise punches, kicks and sweeps. The following features should be developed: commitment and concentration; co-ordination and balance; speed of execution; and control.

Commitment and concentration

As you study the illustrations which follow, make an effort to understand the underlying principles of prospective target areas. When you are satisfied that this has been established, carry out the manoeuvre slowly at first, then as confidence increases try to speed up, aiming to develop snap and power. One good method of improving technique is to practise in front of a large mirror and also with a partner (this is one of the reasons for joining a club). Each technique should be executed with commitment and concentration (ki=spirit).

Co-ordination and balance

Initially the movements of karate feel unnatural. You may look clumsy or lose your balance in attempting them. Try not to become discouraged, but work on the principle that repetition of a well understood technique will eventually lead to a co-ordinated movement. The reason for this is that muscles develop memory so that eventually the action which you are learning becomes almost automatic.

Co-ordination can be improved. One useful exercise should be performed with a partner. Sit opposite each other with your legs interlocked. Each partner then extends the left fist and simultaneously executes alternate right and left hand punches (up to 30). As each punch is thrown the non-punching hand is rapidly withdrawn. This will also improve fitness and balance.

Good balance is acquired by starting each new technique in a controlled manner and never overstretching. It should be remembered that if balance is lost in a contest or street fight you become vulnerable to counterattack, with possible disastrous consequences.

Balancing exercises are an important feature of karate training and can be practised as part of the pre-session warm-up. They should be carried out on a firm, smooth surface.

Balancing exercises

(i) Stand with your feet parallel and hands by your sides; move the left foot and apply the sole to the side of the knee. Hold this position for 5–10 seconds (the neutral position). Now bend forwards from the waist, extending the leg behind you (as a ballet dancer does in an arabesque manoeuvre). If necessary, put your arms out to maintain balance of this position and hold it for 5–10 seconds.
(ii) Return to the neutral position and lean backwards while extending the leg forwards. Hold this position for 5–10 seconds.
(iii) Return to the neutral position and extend the legs sideways using the arms to maintain balance, if necessary. Hold the position for 5–10 seconds and return to neutral.

As expertise increases these exercises can be carried out at speed, eventually pausing only briefly in the neutral position. Remember that all exercises should be carried out using both legs so that co-ordination and balance are equal on both sides of the body.

In punching and blocking techniques balance can be achieved by striking the punch bag, speed ball and padded focus mitts, or working in unison with a partner.

Speed of execution

Speed is usually an inevitable consequence of developing a well balanced, co-ordinated technique, but it can also be apparently increased by the use of distraction or feinting techniques. An example of this would be throwing a fake high punch to the face to distract the opponent's attention and his defence, and following this up immediately with a kick to the body once this has succeeded.

Control

The origins of karate are martial, the end point being effective defence against attack. The techniques which you are learning are potentially dangerous if executed with unmitigated force and you must be aware of this. Learn to develop good control of your punches and kicks by practising regularly against pads, punch bags and partners, withdrawing the blow before full contact is made. You will not be permitted to take part in competition until your control is adequate, otherwise serious injury may result.

Punches

Gyaku-tsuki

This is one of the most powerful hand techniques in karate and is frequently used in competition.

The fighter stands in sochin-dachi (fighting stance), with the left arm extended in knife-hand posture, and the right hand held at the level of the solar plexus just above the belt.

From the get set position the right hand is thrust out at speed while the left hand is simultaneously withdrawn to the side. Note also that power is added to the punch by extending the right leg.

Immediately the punch has been thrown it is withdrawn at speed and the non-punching hand is simultaneously thrust out. This is a defensive manoeuvre which keeps the opponent at arm's length and also prevents him moving in quickly on the defender. The technique of thrusting outwards with the non-punching hand is known as *tate-shuto*. The reverse punch can be directed against the face or the body.

Starting position (sochin-dachi) for the reverse punch (gyaku-tsuki), seen from the front

The hips are thrust forwards as the fist twists at the end of the punch

The hips are pulled back as the non-punching hand is pushed out

The get set position (in some styles of karate students first execute gedan-barai before starting a technique)

Oi-tsuki (the lunge punch)

This technique may also be directed to the face or body. It is executed by gliding forwards with the rear foot and punching with the hand on the same side.

The attacker uses the momentum generated from the rear foot to glide forwards to strike an imaginary opponent to the mid-body

Oi-tsuki demonstrated from the front, showing the mid-point position. The rear foot glides along the floor and the movement does not stop until the punch is completed

Uraken (back fist)

This technique is used to strike the side of an opponent's head or face and may be executed in a manner similar to oi-tsuki as shown or from a jumping position (often having the advantage of considerable surprise).

The mid-point position of uraken. Momentum has been generated, thrusting forwards with the back foot as in oi-tsuki. There is no pause in the mid-point position

The completed strike to an imaginary opponent

After the successful execution of uraken the striking hand is immediately withdrawn

Age-tsuki (rising punch=uppercut)

From the get set position the hips are snapped to the neutral position using the rear leg to supply drive. The non-punching hand is withdrawn sharply and simultaneously with the punching fist which is driven firmly upwards

Kicking techniques

Mae-geri (front kick)

The mid-point of mae-geri. The key to a successful mae-geri is to raise the knee of the kicking foot as high as possible

The leg is then extended sharply and powerfully, the striking surface being the ball of the foot against the chest or face of the imaginary opponent. It is a good idea to practise chudan-level kicks to start with until flexibility of the hips has been developed and the actual technique has been mastered properly

Mawashi-geri (the roundhouse kick)

This is one of the most devastating kicks in karate. Enormous power is generated by rotation of the hips. The roundhouse method of

For mawashi-geri the rear leg (the kicking foot) is raised high and to the side while the hips are rotated

A completed mawashi-geri against the side of the head of an imaginary opponent. The striking surface is the instep of the foot or, alternatively, the ball of the foot with the ankle drawn upwards

delivery also means that the foot approaches an opponent's head from outside his field of peripheral vision, rather like a hooking punch. Defence manoeuvres against the kick are usually too late.

Yoko-geri (side kick)

At the mid-point position for yoko-geri the attacker has rotated on the non-kicking foot, at the same time keeping the knee of the kicking foot high

Further rotation of the non-kicking foot occurs, coupled with powerful extension of the kicking leg. The striking surface is the heel or the side of the kicking foot against the face, head or neck of the imaginary opponent

Mid-way point of a mawashi-geri as seen from the front

Ushiro-geri (back kick)

The get set position (this move can also be started from zenkutsu-dachi)

The attacker rotated on the non-kicking foot through 180 degrees, the direction of rotation being towards the wall, so that she is facing in the opposite direction from the previous one. At this point she also looks backwards to check the target

From the mid-point position the kicking leg is extended towards the target, the striking surface being the heel of the foot

Kakato (heel kick)

The mid-point of kakato. The kicking foot is raised high in the air either perpendicularly or in an ellipse around the opponent

The kicking foot has been raised above the opponent and the heel is then brought crashing downwards on the head, clavicles or trunk (of an opponent who has been swept to the ground)

Mae-ashi-geri (feint front kick converting into full mawashi-geri)

The knee of the kicking foot is raised as if to execute a mae-geri. This posture would encourage an opponent to attempt to counter with either a middle or a lower body block

Observing that the opponent's defence has been breached, the attacker converts immediately to the mid-point posture from mawashi-geri which is then executed to the head

Sweeps

Ashi-barai (the foot sweep)

In this technique the leading or back foot of the opponent is swept away, thus throwing him to the ground. The technique is usually initiated by some sort of feinting manoeuvre to distract his attention and defences.

The get set position for ashi-barai: the fighters face each other. The attacker is on the reader's left

The attacker throws a feint punch to the head, distracting his opponent and drawing his defence. As the attacker moves in, he brings his rear foot in to carry the sweep. Note how the defender has adopted a very narrow and therefore poorly balanced stance

Above **Even our photographer has missed the attacker's right foot sweeping his opponent's left leg away and throwing him to the ground. This shows the sweeping foot returning in preparation for a follow-up attack**

The follow-up attack is with a left gyaku-tsuki to the head of the defenceless opponent

Ushiro-ashi-barai (the reverse foot sweep)

This can be used either as an offensive or a defensive manoeuvre. The following concentrates on its defensive aspects.

Above **The get set position for ushiro-ashi-barai. The attacker stands on the reader's left**

The attacker attempts a right mawashi-geri-chudan which the defender avoids by dropping quickly to the floor, rotating as he does so. Note that the defender keeps a close eye on his opponent at all times

Having dropped to the ground, the defender simultaneously sweeps his opponent's non-kicking leg and throws him heavily to the ground

Tobi-geri (jumping kicks)

These are the kicks of karate legend. They were originally devised to dismount and disable horsemen, but have become an exercise form *per se*. They are an excellent method of developing balance control and co-ordination and should ideally be practised against a target: either a punching bag or, as expertise increases, a focus mitt.

Yoko-tobi-geri

Above **The karateka about to execute the kick stands in the get set position some paces from the focus mitt target. From here the kicker brings her rear foot in front of her leading foot and then, stepping forwards with the right foot, she jumps off the left . . .**

. . . **into a full flying side kick. The striking surface is the heel of the kicking foot**

Note
This is an advanced technique which can only be performed effectively once the basics have been mastered. The whole movement from the get set position to completion of the kick is smooth and fast. As in all karate techniques, the initial practice should be carried out slowly and in steps, which are then fused together.

Tobi-mikzuki-geri (jumping spinning kick)

This is a devastating technique which is difficult to control in competition and should therefore not be used. However, it is an exceptionally useful self-defence technique, especially against an opponent who moves away from an initial attack with a kick.

The attacker executes a mawashi-geri with the leading foot

For the purposes of the exercise it is assumed that in a real combat situation the opponent has moved away as a defensive manoeuvre against the front mawashi-geri. Alternatively, the kick can be used as a combination of a strike with a front mawashi-geri followed up by a further strike with a spinning back kick. Having executed the left mawashi-geri with the leading foot, the kicking foot is brought immediately to the ground and the kicker rotates rapidly, in a clockwise fashion, extending the right leg to strike the focus mitt (or opponent) with the heel of the right foot

BASIC COMBINATIONS

In this section are presented examples of how to combine the basic punches, kicks, sweeps and blocks which have been described in the previous chapters. The aim of these exercises is to establish a repertoire of movements so that one offensive or defensive technique is always followed by another. Thus the intention is to encourage continuous movement forwards in offensive and sideways or backwards in defensive manoeuvres. Concentrate on rhythm, crispness and timing, avoiding jerky or unco-ordinated movements. The basic combinations which follow should comprise part of your weekly training regime.

Low block, haito

Step forwards and execute gedan-barai (low block)

Follow this immediately with a right-handed haito to the imaginary opponent's neck. Return to the starting position

Knife-hand block, front leg roundhouse kick, gyaku-tsuki

Step forward from the get set position into kokutsu-dachi (back stance), carrying out a left shuto-uke (knife-hand block). Note the position (open) of the right hand above the knot of the belt at the level of the solar plexus

Immediately follow this technique with a front leg mawashi-geri to the mid-body of an imaginary opponent

The kicking foot is smartly returned to the ground and the attack is followed up by a right-handed gyaku-tsuki. Return to the starting position

Age-uke (rising block), mae-geri (front kick), gyaku-tsuki (reverse punch)

Step forward executing a left-handed rising block against an imaginary attack to the head. Note that the weight is on the forward foot and that the non-blocking hand has been withdrawn sharply to the side just above the belt. Note also concentration in the fighter's eyes

From the blocking position execute a right mae-geri to the upper chest or head of the imaginary opponent

Follow this up immediately with a right-sided gyaku-tsuki to the middle body; then retreat to the starting position

Soto-uke (outside middle body block), empi (elbow strike)

Step forward and execute a left soto-uke, withdrawing the non-blocking hand rapidly to the level of the belt

Rotate the feet and drop to a low shiko-dachi stance, executing a left empi to the mid-body of an imaginary opponent and at the same time withdrawing the non-striking arm rapidly to the side

Kizami-tsuki, gyaku-tsuki, ushiro-mawashi-geri

Kizami-tsuki (front hand punch)

Kizami-tsuki followed by an immediate right-handed gyaku-tsuki, withdrawing the non-punching hand sharply to the side

The fighter then rotates on the front foot, bringing the right leg up in a semi-circular motion to perform an ushiro-mawashi-geri to the head of the imaginary opponent

Uraken-gyaku-tsuki-mawashi-geri

Step forward bringing up and bending the right elbow in preparation for carrying out the uraken

The completed uraken

The forward hand is
rapidly withdrawn and
the attack is followed up
with a left gyaku-tsuki to
the mid-body

A high left-footed
mawashi-geri is then
executed

Chudan-uke, mawashi-empi (roundhouse elbow strike)

The get set position

Mid-point position in preparation for chudan-uke

Completed chudan-uke

Maintaining the same foot positions, the blocking hand is rapidly withdrawn and a mawashi-empi is executed to the jaw of the imaginary opponent. Return to the get set position

Mae-geri, yoko-geri, ushiro-geri

This is an excellent exercise for combination kicking which can be varied considerably, for instance by practising mae-geri and converting it to mawashi-geri, then ushiro-geri, then yoko-geri, and so on. Note the excellent balance and concentration throughout the exercise.

Right **A mae-geri is executed**

The kicking foot is brought back to the level of the knee and a yoko-geri is performed without allowing the foot to touch the floor

Again the kicking foot is brought to the level of the knee and an ushiro-geri is carried out

SPARRING AND TRAINING

Until now all the techniques you have learned have been against an imaginary opponent or a punchbag. Karate really becomes exciting when training involves sparring with a partner. It is very easy to look good in a mirror or to fight against a punchbag. It is not as easy to be cool and crisp when fighting against someone who can hit back and who may perhaps cause discomfort or injury.

Sanbon-kumite (three-step sparring)

Karate bridges the gap between acquiring basic technique and combinations by a form of prearranged sparring called sanbon-kumite (three-step sparring). In this, one karateka executes three consecutive attacks which are serially blocked by the other. The process is then repeated in reverse. Three-step sparring teaches the fighter to advance while attacking and to retreat, side step or sweep (in more complex forms) while retreating.

The following are some examples of sanbon-kumite.

Basic sparring for beginners

The fighters stand opposite each other. To determine the distance they should stand away from each other, one places his fingers on his opponent's shoulder.

The basic etiquette of bowing to each other is observed, but each fighter brings in his right foot towards the left to avoid clashing of skulls.

To start the sparring the attacker steps backwards and with his right foot he simultaneously carries out a left gedan-barai. The attacker then executes three successive oi-tsukis to the face of his opponent who moves

**Right oi-tsuki-jodan
blocked by jodan-age-uke**

back with each attack, blocking each with a rising block.

The process may be repeated by the other fighter. The manoeuvre is often completed by a counterpunch following the final defence in the form of right gyaku-tsuki-chudan.

A more complex variation of sanbon-kumite

In this combination the attacker performs alternate oi-tsuki-jodan (to the face), then oi-tsuki-chudan (to the body) followed by mae-geri-chudan (front kick to the body). Each attack is countered by the defender who blocks consecutively with jodan-age-uke (rising block), chudan-uchi-uke (inside middle block) then gedan-barai (lower block) to the kick while simultaneously taking a step to the side. The counter is with a right gyaku-tsuki-chudan.

Left oi-tsuki blocked by chudan-uchi-uke

Right mae-geri blocked by gedan-barai with simultaneous sidestep

Counter-attack with right gyaku-tsuki-chudan

Combination three

From the get set position, the fighter on the right attacks with a left oi-tsuki-jodan. The defender steps back and grabs the attacker's forward (punching) hand with her left (nagashi-uke). This defensive manoeuvre is then followed by ushiro-mawashi-geri to the head.

Attack with oi-tsuki-jodan and counter with nagashi-uke. Note that the defender has stepped backwards out of range of the punch

Using her opponent's arm as support, the defender pivots round on her right foot and counter-attacks with a perfect ushiro-mawashi-geri to the head

Ippon-kumite (one-step sparring)

Ippon-kumite consolidates technique. The emphasis is placed on executing single attacks with corresponding defences. The purpose of ippon-kumite is to prepare the fighter for jiyu-kumite (free fighting). Various attacks from kicks to punches are initiated, defended and countered, the aim being to develop quick reactions to unexpected attacks (as would happen in free fighting).

Jiyu-kumite (free fighting)

In free fighting, attacks and defences are performed by both combatants as though an actual fight were taking place. However, great care must be exercised to prevent injury, so kicks or punches are withdrawn just before contact with the target is made. This is an advanced form of kumite which should not be indulged in by novices and it is the basis of modern day competition karate. Free fighting is an important part of the training regime and can be performed towards the end of the training session once the fighters are warm and primed for action.

In general, simple techniques are the most effective in free fighting. You will be able to develop the use of feints or distraction techniques to initiate effective attacks, but a general principle is that the hands are quicker than the feet, that is a good punch will generally score before a kick.

When training for free fighting it is more important to develop fast reactions to your opponent's body movement than to his technique. One method of developing rapid reactions is to alternate between counter-punching and counter-kicking and attacking with your partner. Work in thirty-second spells at full speed. However, the 'attacker' should execute no technique at all but should simply move with his arms at his side sideways, forwards or quickly inwards on his opponent, encouraging him to counter his body movements only. The 'attacker' should change direction as often as possible and try to crowd his opponent, encouraging him to sidestep or move backwards and counter as appropriate. A further useful exercise to develop speed for free fighting and change of direction is to set obstacles on the dojo in a staggered pattern and to pick two teams of karateka to run round the obstacles and return to base as quickly as possible. Time each team against the clock.

Jump kicks from a standing start, jumping back fist attacks, combination kicks and punches are further methods of developing speed and sharpness for competition.

Competition Techniques and Strategy

The following are techniques which have been effective in scoring in competition. Most are executed in less than one second and it is important to realise the continuity of movement which is present. Although each attack or defence involves several stages in practice, some of these stages are almost simultaneous. It is important to remember this during sparring and to practise basic techniques and combinations until they become like reflexes.

Try to develop a competition plan, a flexible strategy of how you will conduct your contest. The success of this plan will obviously depend upon your own physical ability, which you must assess honestly. However, it is also true to say that by harassing or thwarting an attack with a better technique, you can win. Many successful competition fighters are thinking fighters.

Several factors are important in the conduct of the fight. These are: assessing your opponent's abilities; staying on the move; effectively using the fighting area; holding on to a lead; attacking uncompromisingly; feinting techniques.

Assessment of your opponent's abilities

Karate contests are of short duration, lasting only two or three minutes. Therefore you do not have much time to work out what abilities your opponent has; only about 15–20 seconds. Is he a kicker or a puncher? Which is his stronger side? Where are the weaknesses? To answer these questions you should attempt to draw attacks and make decisions about your opponent's reactions. Obviously each contest differs, but it is often possible to decide fairly quickly whether you are dealing with a good kicker or puncher. As you draw the initial attacks and defences, make good use of the fighting area. A useful maxim is to make your opponent look for you. Do not stand and wait to be hit.

Staying on the move

A fighter who stands like a statue is easy to hit. Successful fighters are conspicuous by their free and easy movements. It is also easier to initiate your attacks or defences if you keep moving; it prevents telegraphing your techniques so that you can always retain the element of surprise.

Effective use of the fighting area

Remember that if you leave the fighting area more than three times during a contest you may be penalised. It is therefore important to make as full use of it as possible. Do not allow yourself to be driven into a corner so that the only retreat is out of the area on the one hand or a score by your opponent on the other.

Effective use of the area develops only with competition practice and experience. To acquire this you should watch what other good fighters do and learn from them. As experience increases you will develop a sense of the size of the area even when moving backwards or sidewards (rather like a goalkeeper who can sense the width of the goal-posts behind him even though he cannot see them). Your colleagues and teachers can assist you during competition either by shouting a code or a simple warning that you are about to go out of the area.

Holding on to a lead

Some fighters build up an excellent lead only to lose it all in the last thirty seconds. Several factors may account for this.

(a) Sometimes an inexperienced or junior competitor will find himself in the lead against a fighter whom he felt was superior and in the last thirty seconds the lead may be frittered away by becoming terror struck. If you get into such a position reapply the basic principles which you have learned. Use the area well and remember to keep your opponent chasing you.

(b) Other basic principles are to make use of safe techniques which you feel certain will make him retreat. For instance try to keep out of range all the time so that if your techniques fail, you will not be caught by his counterattack.

(c) Further manoeuvres can also be carried out to maintain a lead such as throwing a mawashi-geri and then falling to the ground, with your feet safely guarding your face and body so that your opponent cannot reach you. This and the use of *jogai* (leaving the area) in the last thirty seconds may be regarded as time wasting by the referee so be careful. Remember it is better to maintain your distance and continue to 'look busy'.

All-out attack

To be effective with all-out attack you need to have good technique, speed and an ability to 'psych out' your opponent. There is no doubt that an aggressive fighter is very difficult to cope with, but remember that there is no problem in counterattacking if the technique is slow and cumbersome.

Attacks with punches

Punches, especially gyaku-tsuki, are excellent scoring techniques in competition, with many advantages over kicks. Firstly, they can be executed much more quickly than kicks. It takes much longer, for instance, to take your foot from the floor to the level of someone's head (no matter how quick you may be) than it does to execute a punch. Secondly, flexibility is not required to the same extent as the shoulder girdle is the most mobile unit in the body. Thirdly, it is easier for most people to use their hands because they gain the necessary skills from performing everyday actions. It is therefore well worthwhile to try practising your punching techniques. The aim is always to be sharper than your opponent so that, during training and sparring practice, you should move in quickly when you see the opening or, alternatively, create the opening yourself by using feinting techniques. The following are some successful examples of competition punching techniques.

Example 1

In this technique you try to make your opponent 'think high'. To do this the attacker adopts a relatively high and narrow stance.

The get set position. Note that the attacker has his right foot forward and that he adopts a narrow stance. This also makes his oponent stand 'tall'

60

The attacker moves forwards slightly with the right foot and drops down quickly

He continues the forward movement with his right foot and executes a left gyaku-tsuki-chudan with the left hand

Example 2

The use of a feint uraken to draw the opponent's defence and counter with gyaku-tsuki.

The attacker has his right foot forward in the get set position

He feints with uraken to the head. This is predictably blocked effectively by his opponent

Immediately the block has begun, the attacker slides in to execute a left-handed gyaku-tsuki-chudan

Uraken attack

In the get set position the attacker has his right foot forward

He attacks with left gyaku-tsuki-chudan which is blocked

Immediately the opponent blocks, the attacker steps quickly to his own right, turning his body as shown to attack with right uraken to the face

Use of head feints to score to the body

In the get set position the attacker stands with his right foot forward

Moving in, he punches to the face with his right hand, which his opponent blocks

Immediately the block has begun, the attacker slips to his own right inside his opponent's defence and punches with a left gyaku-tsuki to the body

Defence against punches

Block and counter of gyaku-tsuki with mae-geri

In the get set position the attacker (left) stands with his left foot forward

He attacks with
gyaku-tsuki and the
defender moves his body
to his own left,
effectively slipping the
punch

The defender
counter-attacks with
mae-geri to the body and
scores

Kicking attacks

Variations on mae-geri

Mae-geri is an effective kick, but if performed in the usual manner it is likely to be blocked. This illustrates how mawashi-geri can be used to draw your opponent's defence and predictable counter with gyaku-tsuki which you, in turn, counter with mae-geri. Both fighters lead with the left foot

The attacker kicks high with a right mawashi-geri (to the side of the head) which is blocked

66

The block is quickly followed up by a counter with right gyaku-tsuki which is short of the target

An almost simultaneous counter is carried out with right mae-geri

Use of mae-geri as a feint

The attacker moves in with a right mae-geri. This draws a low block from his opponent

When the block has been drawn the follow-up is with mawashi-geri-jodan

Attacks with sweeps

Sweeps are the most impressively devastating of all karate techniques and they place your opponent in an extremely vulnerable position.

Learn therefore to follow-up your sweeping manoeuvres quickly because on most occasions ippon will be awarded for a clean sweep and follow-up.

Follow-up of blocked mawashi-jodan with a sweep

In the get set position both fighters stand with their left foot forward

The attacker steps forward with mawashi-geri-jodan, which is blocked

Immediately the block occurs, he changes his attack, bringing his right leg down and into a sweep position

The sweep

The completed sweep and follow-up with gyaku-tsuki

The Meadowbank sweep

This is one of the favourite techniques in the Meadowbank karate club in Edinburgh and has been successfully carried out at international level by many fighters.

In the get set position both fighters stand with their left foot forward

The attacker moves in with gyaku-tsuki to the head to make his opponent move back and narrow his stance

He quickly brings his right hand across his opponent's chest

At the same time his right leg slips behind his opponent's

The sweep is completed with the right leg and right arm moving in opposite directions

The follow-up is with gyaku-tsuki

BREAKING TECHNIQUES (TAMESHIWARI)

We are all familiar with the picture of the karate expert breaking blocks of wood or concrete with his bare hands. In fact it is often dismissed as some kind of illusion, but there is no trickery involved. Even beginners can quickly learn to break wooden or concrete blocks and within a few months will be able to smash stacks of them.

How is this possible? The key is in the forces generated by the technique, whether it be the hand or the foot, and the surface area of the target upon which these forces are concentrated. For example, a gyaku-tsuki executed by a trained karate exponent can reach a velocity of 33–46 feet (10–14 metres) per second and exert a force of around 675 lb (305 kg). When we consider that this is concentrated in a tiny area of the target (the

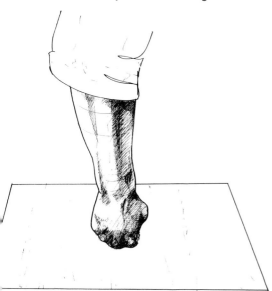

The second and third knuckles only are used to strike the block

striking surface of the hand is the second and third knuckles only) then several kilowatts of power are delivered for a few milliseconds only. This is adequate to break wooden or concrete blocks (or other targets against which punches and kicks are directed, for example, human tissue).

Karate techniques differ from boxing in that the boxer impacts velocity through his punches to a large area on his opponent and this moves him backwards, whereas the karateka aims to stop his technique about a centimetre or two beyond the target and then withdraw. Provided that the hand is held in the correct posture no injury will result because bone is much stronger than either wood or concrete.

Tameshiwari is impressive but it is not the aim of karate. As in all practice, take care in acquiring these skills. If you do not first master the basic techniques then injury is inevitable. Beware, too, of allowing children to practise breaking techniques. Damage to the growth plates of their bones may result and lead to subsequent deformity. As a general rule, tameshiwari should not be taught to children but should be reserved for those over 16 years old.

Materials used

Pine blocks of 30×15cm (12×6in) and 2cm (0.7in) thick are commonly used. They should be dry and smooth.

Concrete slabs usually measure 40×20×4cm (15.75×7.8×1.5in). A useful tip for breaking is to ensure that the material is bone dry. Excess water can be removed by baking them in an oven.

Methods used

1. *Gyaku-tsuki* – peak velocity of 33 feet/sec (10 metres/sec).
2. *Kentsui* – peak velocity of 50 feet/sec (15 metres/sec).
3. *Tegatana* – peak velocity of 50 feet/sec (15 metres/sec).
4. *Mawashi-geri* – peak velocity of 37 feet/sec (11 metres/sec).
5. *Mae-geri* – peak velocity of 50 feet/sec (15 metres/sec).
6. *Yoko-geri* – peak velocity of 50 feet/sec (15 metres/sec).

Striking a block using the side of the hand

The block for breaking should be placed between two supports, held in the hands of a partner or placed on a solid surface with one end raised, usually by the hand of the karateka which also rests on the surface but is protected from it by a towel.

You should then aim to strike the block as near to its centre as possible. Concentrate on generating power and on finishing your techniques through the target. The block will become deformed by the force and will break from the under surface upwards. It has been calculated that it takes almost five times more force to break concrete than to break wood but only a third of the energy. The reasons for this apparent paradox are twofold. Wood deflects and deforms much more than concrete which is brittle. This explains why more energy is required. Secondly, not all of the energy of a karate strike is transferred to the target. This depends on the mass of the target. In the case of wood almost all the energy of the hand is absorbed whereas concrete, being more massive, refuses to accept at least half of it. As mentioned previously, the remainder is absorbed by the hand or foot and is interpreted as pain. Remember, however, that as long as the natural weapon is correctly postured injury will be rare because the bones of the hands and feet can withstand about 1,500 to 2,000 times more force than concrete.

How to practise

Punching and kicking the heavy bag is a useful method of developing enough power for breaking techniques. Initially the bag should be stuffed with sawdust, but as technique and power improve sand may be added to provide more resistance. Although karateka have

Mawashi-geri, ensuring the foot is at right angles to the board

traditionally hardened their fists and feet by punching and kicking straw-padded posts (makiwara) this is not recommended. Punching or kicking the post leads to callus formation of the heads of the knuckles and metatarsal bones of the feet and may predispose the karetaka to arthritis of the related joints in later life. Protective bag mitts should be worn during work on the heavy bag. Your hands will then be less liable to injury, especially if the object for breaking is covered with a cloth to prevent lacerations.

Throughout these training exercises you should concentrate on the correct disposition of the striking hand or foot. Remember that successful tameshiwari depends on the object being struck as near its centre as possible and at right angles to its surface.

SELF-DEFENCE TECHNIQUES

The techniques which you have so far learned will permit you to enjoy karate as a sport. However, because of their inherent dangers, certain techniques such as the karate chop, kakato, jumping kicks, nukite or any attacks to the eyes, throat or testicles are illegal in many karate contests or during free sparring although they may be used in self-defence situations.

Self-defence differs from sport karate in that you are not being judged by a referee for artistry or excellence of technique. There are no rules. You are confronted with one or more people who intend to inflict physical injury on you or even kill you. Often there is a choice of 'flight or fight'. If there is an opening for you to run away it is wisest to do so. There is no loss of face from running away from trouble on the street. It is only when there is no other option that you should choose to fight.

Unfortunately, there is increasing evidence that attacks against the person are becoming more common. Women are especially vulnerable to attacks on the streets, particularly when returning home late, for example, from a party or a discotheque. The attacks often happen near home and are frequently committed by a person who is known to the victim, who lives in the same area or who travels in the same direction to work. Some of the attacks happen after weeks of 'shadowing' by the assailant. Others occur on the spur of the moment. Many are for sexual reasons. Women should be aware of these unpleasant possibilities and would be well advised to arrange to return home with friends, avoiding poorly lit streets or desolate parks whenever possible. One important thing to remember when faced with an impending attack or even during an attack is to keep as cool as possible, making every effort to get away either by force or by guile. There is substantial evidence that shouting, 'Fire!' or 'Stop thief!' is more likely to attract the attention of passers-by than shouting 'Rape!'. There are also well-documented cases of female college students avoiding rape by agreeing to sexually satisfy their assailant by some other method. Unpleasant though this alternative is, it may prevent rape or murder and should only be resorted to in the face of overwhelming threat. It may also buy time for the woman to plan an escape or even get help.

Men are also the subject of urban violence. Attacks range from pub fights and arguments over parking spaces to ambushes by one or several assailants. It is important to remember how volatile people can be. Again, if possible it is always better to stay calm and walk or run away, using self-defence methods only if all the alternatives fail or if it is obvious that a fervent attack has been launched.

Use of skills outside the dojo

There are legal implications to possessing self-defence skills. The use of violence will only be condoned if you are defending yourself, you are defending others, or there is extreme danger with no other means of retreat.

The force used by you must be the minimum required to repudiate the attack. Although the measure of retaliation is not exactly specified, it should be roughly equivalent to the attack of your assailant, for example if you are attacked by punches or kicks an equivalent form and amount of force is expected from you by the courts. Allowances would also be made for your fear or excitement and may mitigate in your favour should your would-be assailant end up in hospital and then, paradoxically, take *you* to court for assault! In such a situation a completely untrained person might well be allowed a greater degree of error in his assessment of the effect of a blow than you with your karate skills.

As an example of the principle the tale of 'tadpole' and 'toad' may serve you well.

1. 'Tadpole' is 16 years old and is very slightly built for his age. He has, however, been attending karate classes for three or four years, has done quite well in competition, but has never been involved in any 'real-life' fights.

2. 'Toad' is an extremely well-built 19-year-old who is quite well known in the area, and is certainly known to Tadpole as a weight-lifter of some considerable note.

3. Toad is at a disco and is slightly (but not very) drunk. For some reason, apparently quite unjustifiably, he takes a dislike to Tadpole.

4. Outside Toad hurls verbal abuse at Tadpole who, quite sensibly (in view of his size in relation to Toad), simply does not reply and makes to clear off.

5. This seems to annoy Toad, who runs up behind Tadpole and pinions his arms. In law, at this point Toad has inflicted a criminal assault on Tadpole.

6. Because of Toad's strength his action is extremely painful for Tadpole, who quite cleverly screams loudly and causes Toad to release his hold to try to silence him. Tadpole, managing to divert Toad's attention momentarily by stamping on his foot, runs off. In law, Tadpole has not been guilty of an assault in stamping on Toad's foot. He has not in any way used excessive force, and he has done the right thing in running away.

7. Tadpole runs up an alley to get to another street, but because of work being carried out on a gas pipe there is a high temporary hoarding blocking off the alley. Toad quickly catches up with Tadpole.

8. Tadpole is in a state of considerable fear and alarm, for he is now cornered. Remember, he has never been in a fight before in spite of his karate skills and Toad is extremely powerful.

9. Toad, even more annoyed with Tadpole and still slightly inebriated, advances towards Tadpole. Since he does not in any way rate Tadpole as an opponent because he is so small, he simply strolls leisurely up to him.

10. Tadpole, however, has realised that he is going to be assaulted, and has decided to endeavour to use his skills to protect himself. Completely to Toad's surprise, Tadpole lands a very severe blow to his leg, which causes Toad to fall to the ground in considerable pain.

11. This leaves the way clear for Tadpole to escape, but surprised and really rather pleased at himself, he does not do so.

12. Toad is trying to get up, still in pain, and is now more concerned with his leg than with Tadpole. The inevitable onlookers have arrived.

13. Tadpole, flushed with his success, and no doubt spurred on by an audience, proceeds to land further blows on Toad who, much to the onlookers' astonishment (and no doubt Toad's) is completely unable to defend himself. He is, within a very short time, senseless.

14. Tadpole leaves the scene. Toad is fortunately not seriously injured. He is bruised about the body and, more seriously for his weight-lifting, has a dislodged knee-cap.

15. Analysing the position in law, we would point out that Tadpole did not commit any actionable assault the first time he struck Toad. He did not, under the circumstances, use unnecessary force, but it was that blow that did the serious damage. Had it not been justified it could well have given rise to a civil damages claim because of the potential long-term effects on Toad's weight-lifting. Thereafter, however, Tadpole could and should have made his escape. The blows he subsequently inflicted were undoubtedly criminal assaults on Toad, even though Toad had been the original aggressor, and while Tadpole could have pleaded *provocation* in mitigation, each blow he struck would make that less and less of a possibility.

16. In the event, although the police became involved, Toad prevailed upon them not to pursue charges – no doubt because he was the instigator of the incident and also probably because his pride was considerably hurt.

However, if you use more than the minimum force necessary to defend yourself you may not be so fortunate.

Weapons used in self-defence

The most effective weapon is that which deals with the attack as soon as possible and is directed against your opponent's most vulnerable area. Part of your everyday karate practice should be self-defence techniques. If you practise them they are more liable to be effective in a real attack.

The most powerful weapon is the foot and leg and should be used wherever possible. The leg is longer than the arm and will outreach an assailant's punch. Direct your kicks low to the shins, thighs, groin or abdomen of your attacker. Low kicks are less likely to be grabbed and may buy the few vital seconds it takes to get away or run for help.

When an assailant grabs you it may not always be possible to use long kicks but stamping (on his feet) or upward drives with the knee (into his groin) are effective counters, especially if followed up with a throw or lock.

Everyday articles may also be used as weapons, for example an umbrella, a heavy handbag, hair-spray or deodorant, stiletto heels. In fact, one elderly woman having successfully dispatched a 'mugger' informed the newspaper reporter interviewing her that 'A girl should never be without a long hat-pin'. Perhaps she is right!

Security whistles or sirens can also be purchased. These emit a loud continuous sound rather like a car-alarm and may be of value in attracting attention. They have the disadvantage of having to be set off.

Examples of attack situations

Breaking grips on the wrist

Defence against a wrist-grab

A fairly common place for attacks is the connecting pathways between built-up areas.

A girl makes her way along such a route only to be grabbed by a passer-by. An element of surprise and speed are features of successful defence. As soon as the victim's wrist is grabbed she immediately rotates it, palm upwards, placing the other hand firmly behind the wrist crease of her assailant and thrusting firmly upwards. If this is done quickly enough his grip will be released giving her the opportunity to escape.

Defence against a crossover wrist-grab

The right wrist is grasped. As soon as this happens the victim twists her right hand round so that it grasps the attacker's wrist. At the same time the victim brings her left hand over the attacker's hand and wrist, embedding her elbow in the elbow crease of the attacker and exerting firm downward pressure.

The attacker grabs the victim's right wrist

The victim twists her right hand and grasps the attacker's wrist

Countering attacks from the front

Attempted double hand choke

The victim is attacked from the front. The assailant attempts to choke her. The victim immediately steps backwards with the left foot while raising the right arm. This is followed by a rapid drop of her body-weight as she turns to her left, during which time the victim grasps her attacker's right hand with her left. Another rapid change in body position follows as she drives forwards with the right leg and strikes her attacker's face or neck with her right elbow.

She turns to her left and she takes hold of the attacker's right hand

The attacker is trying to strangle his victim

She moves in forwards with empi to the attacker's neck

Single-handed choke

If grabbed from in front, the victim should step in towards the attacker, pushing his arm away with the left hand while simultaneously striking him in the groin with the right hand or knee.

She quickly steps back

79

Countering attacks from behind

At arm's length

If grasped at arm's length from behind, the victim should turn around and grab the attacker's hand with his right and apply his left to the attacker's elbow joint. The victim should also push the attacker's wrist backwards, continuing to apply pressure to the elbow until the attacker is forced to the ground.

Around the neck

The attacker here attempts to pull his victim backwards. The victim can counter this by scraping her heel down the attacker's shin or stamping on his foot. The victim then steps sideways to her right or left, as appropriate, drops her hips and rotates to the opposite side, holding on to the attacker's arm. The attacker will be thrown heavily to the ground.

Good execution of an arm lock: pressure is exerted on the wrist and just above the elbow joint

Countering an attack with a weapon

Remember, as in all defence manoeuvres, that if there is an opportunity to run away you should always take it as your first option.

Attack with scissors or knife

The attacker attempts to stab his victim in the abdomen with a pair of scissors

The defender sidesteps and blocks the attack outwards with his right forearm

Grabbing the arm and wrist with both hands, the defender moves them upwards and over in a circular motion, throwing the attacker to the ground

Maintaining hold of the hand with the weapon, he then stamps on the rib cage (or neck if the attacker does not release the scissors)

VULNERABLE AREAS OF THE HUMAN BODY

All students of karate should be aware of the potential implications of the techniques which they learn. It is therefore important to know the vulnerable areas of the human body so that· they can be avoided during sparring and competition (i.e. the blows controlled) or attacked whole-heartedly in a life or death self-defence situation. Knowledge of the positions of vital organs will help referees to score techniques and may also give an indication of the type of injury which can be

anticipated if someone gets hurt during competition.

In the following diagrams many of the sites will be familiar. Study them closely. The most appropriate attacks are also listed.

1. The head

The most vulnerable areas are the crown and the temples, although any technique which

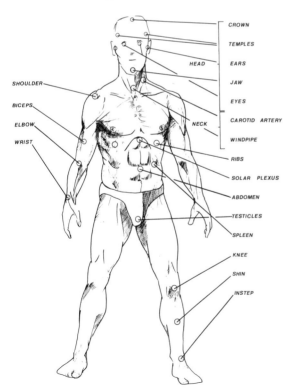

Pressure points on the front of the body

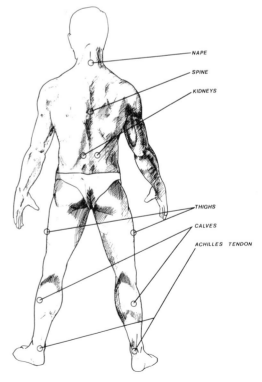

Pressure points on the back of the body

accelerates the head will lead to brain movement and subsequent knockout or haemorrhage. Rotational attacks, i.e. hooking punches and roundhouse kicks, are especially liable to produce shearing forces between the layers of the brain and may cause extensive damage.
Ideal attacks: kentsui, uraken, kakato, mawashi-geri.

2. The ears

Strikes to the ears can be extremely painful. They may also lead to deafness due to rupture of the ear-drums.
Ideal attacks: uraken, the palms of the hands, mawashi-geri.

3. The jaw

Hook punches and kicks exert rotational forces on the spinal cord and brain which lead to the shearing of nerve fibres and knockout. Straight attacks may produce a 'contre-coup' brain injury. This means that the brain is injured on the opposite side from where the blow made contact. The reason is brain movement caused by the technique, for example a punch to the chin, may cause injury to the back of the brain.
Ideal attacks: all punches, empi, mawashi-geri, reverse mawashi-geri.

4. The eyes

Remember that no matter how big an attacker is he becomes infintely less dangerous if he cannot see.
Ideal attacks: nukite, uraken, single fingers.

5. Nape of the neck

This is a well-known vulnerable spot open to attack from the schoolboy 'rabbit punch'.
Ideal attacks: kentsui, tegatana, mawashi-geri, ushiro-mawashi-geri.

6. Side of the neck

This is a highly vulnerable area due to the important structures – the carotid artery, the internal jugular vein and the vagus nerve (stimulation of which slows or stops the heart) – which pass through it.
Ideal attacks: punches, empi, kentsui, tegatana, mawashi-geri.

7. Trachea (the windpipe)

This is extremely vulnerable. A firm blow will disable the strongest opponent because it causes swelling of the larynx (voice box) and difficulty with breathing.
Ideal attacks: punches, empi, tegatana, hiza, mawashi-geri, mae-geri (if the opponent is on the ground).

8. The sternum (breast bone)

All out attack may cause fractures or internal damage to heart and lungs.
Ideal attacks: punches, empi, hiza, kicks.

9. The solar plexus

Situated just below the rib-cage in the midline, the solar plexus is well known to boxers as the area which produces 'winding'. When struck the victim has difficulty inspiring air.
Ideal attacks: punches, empi, hiza, kicks.

10. The ribs

Any area of the rib cage is vulnerable to attacks. In the upper chest-wall blows can cause broken ribs or damage to the heart and lungs. Lower down, blows to either side may rupture the liver, the spleen or the kidneys.
Ideal attacks: straight punches, empi, mawashi-geri, mae-geri.

11. The spine

Direct blows to any area of the neck and spine can cause dislocation of the vertebra, with paralysis or death ensuing, depending on the level of injury.
Ideal attacks: kentsui, mawashi-geri.

12. The upper arm

If struck firmly in the middle third, damage to the radial nerve will result. This produces weakness or paralysis of the grip and is a frequent target when faced with an attacker who is carrying a weapon.
Ideal attack: mawashi-geri.

13. The elbow joint, shoulder and wrist

These are all vulnerable to injury if forced beyond their normal range.
Ideal attacks: locks against the joint (elbow, wrist) mawashi-geri (shoulder – may cause dislocation).

14. The abdomen

All punches and kicks can cause damage to the internal organs (*see* solar plexus).

15. The testicles

Well-known to most as extremely vulnerable!
Ideal attacks: all punches, hiza, mae-geri, ushiro-geri.

16. The knee joint

Vulnerable to dislocation from direct attacks.
Ideal attack: stamp kick.

17. The shin

The tibia lies just under the shin. Blows lead to lacerations and exquisite pain.
Ideal attacks: mae-geri, stamp kick, heel scrape (*see* self-defence techniques).

18. The instep

Vulnerable to all stamping attacks especially with stiletto heels.
Ideal attacks: stamp kicks, preliminary to a throw.

19. The Achilles tendon

The rope-like structure connecting the calf muscles to the heel bone. Injury or rupture will disable an opponent, making him unable to walk.
Ideal attack: stamp kick from behind.

20. The thighs/muscles of the calf

All soft tissues are vulnerable to trauma. Haemorrhage and bruising will ensue. Direct kicks to the thigh lead to 'dead-leg' and temporary immobility during which time further attacks can be launched. Alternatively, you can make your getaway.
Ideal attack: mawashi-geri.

Note Striking the vulnerable areas with unmitigated force can cause serious injury and death. Do not 'try out' your techniques on people just to see the result. Learning karate confers a heavy responsibility which must be adhered to. Full contact must only be used to allow escape from a potentially dangerous situation.

PREVENTION AND MANAGEMENT OF INJURIES

Injury situations

Being by its very nature a combat sport, karate can produce injury. However, it is sometimes difficult to see how this can be prevented, as part of the original philosophy of karate is to accept pain stoically, without complaint.

Injuries in training

Almost everyone who does physical exercise will at some time develop aches, pains or stiffness. These are all acceptable. More serious overuse injuries can result if you overtrain and you should be aware of these. The real problem arises when injuries are sustained because of overcrowding, poor lighting or poor floor surfacing. Such injuries can usually be prevented. You and your coach or sensei have the ability to change this and prevent injury, even if it means that several more members of the class stay seated while others spar or train.

Injuries in competition

In the numerous studies which we have carried out, injury occurs more commonly in the lower grade fighters who have not yet developed adequate control over their techniques, and who are often rather excited or nervous, making them prone to accidents. It is also the case that novices tend to get injured at the beginning of the day's contest.

Remember that karate is a game, bound by rules and regulations by which you must abide. While in competitions it is the referee who controls the contest, his decisions must be supported by the governing body, which is therefore ultimately responsible for preventing injury. To this end the Martial Arts Commission, recognised by the Sports Council as the controlling body for the martial arts, is advised by specialist medical experts who put safety recommendations to the Commission at regular intervals and review injury statistics. In this manner karate has gradually become a safer sport and serious injury is now rare.

Prevention of injury

Both teachers of combat sports and competition organisers are aware of their social and legal obligations to their students. The following guidelines have been effective in reducing injuries in training and/or competition.

1. A medical certificate of fitness to fight should be presented if a fighter has any previous history of a major serious illness.
2. Each fighter should carry a fight record card in which previous performances and injuries are recorded.
3. Medical cover is essential at all competitions.
4. After an injury to eye, ear or head the competitor should be examined medically before fighting again. A minimum period of four weeks should elapse after a head injury. During this time the fighter can train but should not be allowed to spar.
5. Equivalent weight classes should be encouraged. Ideally, no fighter should outweigh his opponent by more than 7lb (3kg).
6. Referees, coaches and karate teachers should be encouraged to learn first aid and it should form an integral part of grading.

7. The governing body should issue a summary of the rules of the sport which should be readily available to all members of the association.

8. A summary of the rules should be announced before each competition.

9. Suitable protective equipment in the form of fist, foot and shin pads should be worn as recommended by the governing body. Gum shields (custom built by your dentist) are to be encouraged. Groin guards are mandatory and padded or protective brassières are beneficial.

10. Dangerous manoeuvres should be banned. Such techniques may include kakato, the spinning back kick and the jumping back kick.

Minor illnesses

At some time during training most fighters will be affected by a cold or a 'flu-like illness with upper respiratory tract symptoms such as a runny nose, a minor cough or possibly a spit. This might also be accompanied by muscular aches and pains associated with headaches and possibly even nausea or vomiting. All these signs must be taken seriously for it has been shown beyond doubt that minor infections, especially those of a viral nature, can produce inflammation of the covering of the heart which may cause cardiac arrest during strenuous exercise, irrespective of how fit an athlete is. This is one cause of sudden death in sport. The wisest preventive measure is therefore not to train at all when suffering from a cold or 'flu, or only to take part in very light, non-strenuous exercise.

Common injuries

Face, head and neck

Lacerations, abrasions, nose bleeds and black eyes were once common but are less so now that control and protective pads are used, especially in competition.

Head injuries must be taken seriously. Any person who becomes confused after a blow to the head should be examined by a doctor *as soon as possible*. Normal training can be resumed after a minor head injury, but sparring or competition should be avoided for at least four weeks to prevent the risk of further injury and damage.

If a fighter reports numbness, tingling or weakness of a limb after a blow to the head or neck, medical advice should be sought. If there is paralysis of the arms or legs after an uncontrolled contact *do not move* the injured person until expert help is available. Call an ambulance.

Injuries to the trunk

Winding from blows to the solar plexus (midriff) is the most common trunkal injury. Recovery is rapid and serious complications are uncommon. However, if a person continues to feel unwell after several minutes, the doctor should be alerted or the person should be transported to a hospital. Testicular injury most commonly results from foul play, and paradoxically it is the victim who is disqualified for not wearing his groin guard. The message from this is quite clear.

Injuries to the limb

Finger and thumb injuries are common and fracture of the knuckle bones or base of the thumb can occur. These injuries should be treated at a hospital. Major joint dislocation is uncommon in karate and the only real instance is following an extremely heavy contact in the shoulder region.

Nerve injuries occur in the arm and the leg and produce tingling and weakness. No further treatment is required unless symptoms persist. However, remember too that tingling and weakness of a limb may be associated with a neck injury. It is always wise to ask for a medical opinion in such cases.

Principles of immediate management

Although prevention is effective, at some time you may sustain an injury. Early and correct management provides the best basis for a speedy recovery. It can also prevent the onset of later complications and may even save lives in serious injuries.

It has been stated that injuries will occur either in training or in the course of a competition. The best way to prepare for such an eventuality is to learn basic first aid. This knowledge can be acquired by enrolling at one of the courses run by the British Red Cross Society, the St John Ambulance Association and Brigade or the St Andrew's Ambulance Association or by reading a book they have jointly produced called *First Aid*. The Martial Arts Commission has also organised annual weekend courses, throughout the country, relating first aid to combat sports. Other sources of information include their booklet *First Aid for the Martial Artist* which is available from the Commission. Some further texts are *KTG Sports Injuries*, and the Scottish Sports Council pamphlet entitled *Sports Injuries – How to Help*.

Crucial Decisions

A doctor should be present at competitions. This relieves coaches from much of the responsibility. However, if no doctor is present, you may have to decide what to do, and in order to do so you should ask yourself the following questions.

1. Is the injured person fit to continue fighting?
2. Does he need to see a doctor?
3. Is he fit to continue/restart training?

Urgency

Depending on your knowledge and the severity of the injury you must decide whether to manage without professional help or get the injured person to a doctor. There are three degrees of urgency.

1. *See a doctor as soon as possible*. This means immediately. Serious injury may require ambulance transport.
2. *See a doctor the same day*. In this situation, if the person is fighting away he can return to his home town to be seen by a doctor. The problem is less urgent.
3. *See a doctor but make an appointment*.

Some injuries do not need to be seen the same day. For these it is sufficient simply to make an appointment to see a doctor. This will apply to most minor sprains and strains.

The RICE principle

The **RICE** principle is an effective and safe way of managing soft tissue injuries.

R = Relative rest. The injured part may need complete rest. More often, by cutting back on training or changing to another type of exercise, physical fitness can be maintained while the injury recovers.
I = Ice. Ice reduces the amount of bleeding and bruising. It also reduces pain. Be careful not to burn the skin by applying it for too long.
C = Compression. After applying ice for 10–30 minutes intermittently, apply a firm bandage to the area if possible. This will further prevent bleeding and swelling.
E = Elevation. If a limb is injured, elevation of the injured part will also assist in reducing the swelling.

When an injury occurs, however, the following procedures should be observed.

1. **Look.** Look at the injured part. Is there deformity or bleeding? Is there bruising or swelling?
2. **Listen.** Listen to what the injured person has to say. Does what he say make sense? Does he know what happened? This is especially important for head injuries.
3. **Ask.** Ask the injured person if he can move the affected part, for example, an injured limb, without your assistance.
4. **Stay cool.** It was stressed earlier that you must stay in control during a fight. The same principle applies to injuries. In front of a crowd of 2,000 people or more this may be difficult. Try to reassure the injured person and always explain anything that you are going to do. The best way of staying cool is to have a sound basic knowledge of first aid.
5. **Touch and feel.** After you have acquired the preceding information it may not be necessary to touch the injured part. However, if you do, you should compare it with the uninjured limb

and gently feel the injured area. Is it tender? Is it swollen?

Soft tissue injuries

Injuries to the skin, muscles, tendons and joint ligaments are the commonest, and will account for more than 80 per cent of all karate injuries. Many occur during competition but some are caused by overtraining.

Remember, too, that the tissues in the brain, the eyes, the heart, the lungs and the abdominal muscles are regarded as soft tissues. These will also be dealt with.

Skin injuries

Lacerations

Ragged cuts result from uncontrolled punches. Clean the area with a disinfectant solution such as Dettol. Cover with a dressing and, if extensive, refer to hospital on the same day.

Bruises

A bruise is due to bleeding under the skin. It will settle with time, becoming progressively discoloured. To alleviate pain and prevent further swelling, apply a cold compress – either ice or a cold pack. Protect the skin with a towel to prevent ice burns. Apply at intervals of ten minutes.

Abrasions

When friction is applied to the skin a friction burn or abrasion is the result. Often a fluid called serum leaks from it. Gently clean it with disinfectant. If there is ingrained dirt it should be treated at Casualty because unsightly tattooing can result. Transport the person to hospital, covering the wound with a dry, non-stick dressing.

Blisters

These are very common. The friction forces between foot and floor are very great during a fight. Blisters are therefore found most often on the feet. Treat them by puncture with a sterile needle, apply a strapping to prevent further injury, and allow the fighter to continue. If there has been skin loss, cut the excess away with scissors. Gently clean with disinfectant and if the fighter wishes to continue apply strapping.

Remember, if the skin has been broken there is a risk of tetanus (lockjaw) infection. This can be prevented. Make certain that the fighter's tetanus immunisation is up to date by visiting your GP or the Accident and Emergency Department at your local hospital within 24 hours of injury.

Muscle injuries

Punches or kicks are the commonest causes of this type of injury. However, since the fibres can also be torn during stretching exercises you should remember to warm up slowly.

The large muscles of the thigh, the biceps in the arm or the pectoral muscles on the chest are sometimes injured by punches or kicks. Bleeding occurs which produces pain and tenderness. Apply an ice pack. Do not rub or massage muscle injuries.

During warm-up or stretching both the hamstring muscles on the back of the thigh and the adductors on the inside of the legs can be torn.

Tendon injuries

These are uncommon karate injuries, but ones which can occur if a lot of running is done as a part of training. In such instances the tendon becomes inflamed from overuse and is tender to touch. Movement will also cause pain.

Rupture of tendons is due to direct injury. Although rare it can occur as a freak injury in overcrowded training areas.

Ligament injuries

The ligaments in the knee, the ankle, the toes and the fingers are all prone to injury in karate. They may be sprained or torn completely. A sprain is a partial tear.

Injuries to bones and joints

A broken bone is called a fracture. Look to see if there is deformity and if the person can move the injured limb. Ask if it is very painful. Feel the area to see if there is swelling or if it is locally tender. Do this very gently.

It may be necessary to splint the injured limb. It is advisable to learn how suspected fractures should be immobilised. Dislocations occur most often to the fingers and toes. If seen immediately there is obvious deformity, try once to pull the digit straight. If unsuccessful, take the person to hospital.

Special groups

Children in competition

Children under the age of 16 are not responsible for decisions regarding their own safety. Therefore any child who joins your club must have parental consent and must be carefully supervised at all times. While it is quite permissible to allow children to take part in competition, they should certainly not be expected to perform feats of strength such as wood breaking, press-ups on the knuckles or any hardening techniques of the hands which can lead to damage of the growing joints. Your club may eventually be legally obliged to compensate for such injuries if reasonable care has not been taken.

During children's competitions there is generally a high degree of excitement and anxiety on the part of the competitors themselves. As a referee or organiser of such a competition you must therefore do your utmost to forewarn the children that observing the rules is all-important. It is almost inevitable that control will be poor in such contests. Keep a tight rein and you will reduce injuries to a minimum.

Women in combat sport

This text has been written for both men and women who take part in combat sports. During the last five years large numbers of women have taken part in both competition karate and in self-defence classes and the reasons for this are an increased awareness of the risk of attack in the street and a genuine wish to improve fitness. Also, like men, female competitors have discovered the excitement and satisfaction of practising karate and participating in competition. All the available evidence points to the fact that women increase their strength, just like men, with training, and there is even some evidence to suggest that women may be capable of acquiring greater endurance than males.

Special precautions

1. Always wear a gum shield.
2. Long hair should be kept well under control, so that it does not fall over your face and eyes.
3. Nails should be short and no jewellery should be worn.
4. Breast protection for women is recommended, although some of the breast guards currently on the market are uncomfortable. It is therefore acceptable to wear either a tight-fitting brassière or a fairly tight vest to control breast movement during competition. If a woman sustains a blow to the breast and subsequently feels a lump, she should see her doctor.
5. Groin injuries, lacerations, or bruises of the vulva and vagina in women, may result from wayward kicks. Some form of groin protection should be worn whether it is a groinbox or, for women, just a sanitary towel.

Personal hygiene

Keep your kit clean and you will avoid the risk of infection from such fungi as cause athlete's foot or 'jock itch'. These conditions, which are highly infectious, present themselves as an itch between the toes or in the groin crease. The fungus spreads by direct contact with floors, contaminated clothing, and so on. Most surfaces can in fact harbour the infection and spread it from person to person. Do not share towels, wear a dirty groin guard or use the same towel all week, as all these things can contribute to the problem.

Advice for prevention of fungus infections

1. Have two or even three sets of training gear so that one is always regularly cleaned. If you only have one set, make sure it is washed at least twice a week.
2. Wash your feet at least once a day and certainly after each training session. Do not soak them for long periods. Dry them gently, leaving them exposed for several minutes before putting on your socks, which should be changed daily. Talcum powder, although refreshing, is not a substitute for proper drying, especially between the toes.

Treatment

It is best to treat athlete's foot with an antifungal preparation such as Mycil or Tinaderm. These are available from chemists without prescription. Athlete's groin can be treated in a similar fashion.

Verrucas and corns

Foot warts (verrucas) are fairly common. They produce a feeling of walking on a pebble. They require specialised treatment from a chiropodist or a doctor. If the condition persists, you should only be allowed to train wearing light plimsoles in order to avoid spreading the infection. You should also wear plastic sandals in the shower or you should bathe separately.

A corn is a thickening of the normal skin and results from friction at pressure points. Treatment is with lanolin or abrasion with an emery board.

Remember also to keep your toe-nails short and clean. If dirty and long they can produce cuts which may become infected.

Miscellaneous

Alcohol and training

Alcohol comprises about ten per cent of the average weekly carbohydrate intake of the British adult. There is no doubt that one or two drinks will not unnecessarily hamper athletic performance, but if a high standard of excellence is being sought, alcohol should be cut out of training altogether.

Sex

There is no evidence at all that sexual activity before an event impedes performance. Some athletes boast that it considerably improves theirs. The most important thing is not to stay up late on a night before a contest.

Drugs

Stimulants and anabolic steroids are illegal in most countries. Biochemical methods for detecting these substances have improved markedly, and random testing is a standard technique. Drug taking is a form of cheating which cannot be recommended. In many cases it is a dangerous pastime and in the long term can damage your health.

Responsibilities

If you organise, judge or referee a karate competition, you have specific responsibilities. For instance, you are responsible for ensuring that reasonable safety precautions are taken in competition. This should include the provision of padded flooring or, if this is not available, sprung flooring, as well as ensuring that competitors are correctly clad and wearing sufficient protective padding. You should provide a well-equipped first-aid box and make sure that there is a member of the club, either a trainer or instructor, who is competent in its use. This skill can only be acquired by attending basic first-aid classes.

In general terms, then, karate should be controlled in the following manner.

1. Teachers should be adequately qualified.
2. Participants should be 'screened' to ensure that they are fit to undertake strenuous exercise. This could be done quite simply by asking whether the kareteka suffers from any serious conditions/diseases for which he has to attend a doctor.
3. Adequate facilities for training should be available.
4. Adequate medical back-up should be available.

Major emergencies

The techniques described in this section are life saving. In order to become skilled in their use you need the sort of specialist training which can be obtained from first-aid courses. Training is also available through Medimac. Write to the Martial Arts Commission, 15 Deptford Broadway, London SE8 4PE for details of courses.

The British Association of Trauma in Sports/Basics programme (BASIC=Basic Athletic/Sports Injury Care) may be useful. The association comprises a body of doctors which runs courses on a regional basis for lay people involved in sport. The management of all sports related injuries is covered from soft tissue bruising to major emergencies, and mock injury situations are demonstrated. For details write to: The Secretariat (BATS), 110 Harley Street, London.

Immediate emergency action

How to clear the airway

After an accident more people die from suffocation than from broken bones. If a competitor is unconscious after a blow, clear his airway. To do this remove false teeth and debris from the mouth and gently extend the neck. Check that the person is breathing after you have done this.

The carotid pulse

Located on both sides of the windpipe, the carotid artery is easily felt. Press gently with your fingers on either side of your windpipe and feel the pulsation. The pulse is the best indicator of whether or not the heart is beating and should always be examined if a cardiac arrest is suspected.

The coma position

If the injured person is breathing spontaneously, place him in the coma position. This prevents him from inhaling vomit, broken teeth or blood.

The 'five-man lift'

When a neck injury is suspected it may be necessary to lift the patient on to a stretcher. Special training and practice is required for this manoeuvre which is only necessary if expert help is unavailable (that is, hours away).

Cardio-pulmonary resuscitation (CPR)

If the airway is clear but there is no breathing, artificial respiration is required. This should be mouth-to-mouth. If the carotid pulse is absent then CPR must be started.

Sites of major abdominal organs

The liver, the stomach, the spleen and the right and left kidneys are all organs which are vulnerable to injury. Control should therefore be exercised in abdominal blows to these areas, and high scores should be awarded for successful and controlled attacks.

How to deal with cardiac arrest

If a cardiac arrest is suspected, the following steps should be taken.

1. Feel the carotid pulse in the neck. Is it present?
2. If no pulse can be felt, clear the airway by gently extending the neck.
3. Give the breast bone a firm thump with the side of the fist.

4. Sharply compress the breast bone four times with the heels of both hands.
5. Inflate the lungs by pinching the person's nose and firmly exhaling into his mouth.
6. Compress the chest four times.
7. Inflate the lungs, watch the chest inflate.
8. Compress the chest four times.

Continue this procedure until help arrives. To become efficient at this life-saving technique, you should enrol in a first-aid course both if you have never attended one or if it has been more than five years since you were last on a course.

FURTHER READING

Other martial arts books from A & C Black:

Elite Karate Techniques (David Mitchell)

EP Sport Judo (Geof Gleeson)

Health and Fitness in the Martial Arts (Dr J.C. Canney)

Judo Games (Geof Gleeson)

Judo Inside Out (Geof Gleeson)

Junior Martial Arts (Tony Gummerson)

Know the Game Judo (Geof Gleeson)

Know the Game Karate (The Martial Arts Commission)

The Martial Arts Coaching Manual (David Mitchell)

Okinawan Karate (Mark Bishop)

Self Defence for All (Fay Goodman)

Books on injury and first aid

First Aid, Joint Publication of the British Red Cross Society, the St John Ambulance Association and the St Andrew's Ambulance Association.

First Aid for the Martial Artist, J. Canney and D. Mitchell, available from The Martial Arts Commission, Broadway House, 15 Deptford Broadway, London SE8 4PE.

Sports injuries 'How to help', G. McLatchie and D. Macleod. Available from the Scottish Sports Council, 1 St Colme Street, Edinburgh.

Know The Game Sports Injuries, Vivian Grisogono, A & C Black.

APPENDIX

A typical example of a grading syllabus

9th Kyu (red)

lower block × 5,	forwards then	backwards rising block × 5
face punch × 5,	forwards then	backwards outside block × 5
stomach punch × 5,	forwards then	backwards inside block × 5
front kick × 5,	forwards then	turn front kick × 5
side snap kick × 3,	forwards then	turn side snap kick × 3

Kata – taikyoku shodan
3-step sparring
Exercises – Women: 5 press ups   Men: 10 press ups
10 sit ups   10 sit ups
10 squat thrusts   10 squat thrusts

8th Kyu (orange)

The same applies as for the 9th Kyu, with the exception of shuto uke (knife-hand block in back stance).
Kata – heian shodan
3-step sparring: jodan, chudan, mae-geri
Exercises – Women: 5 press ups   Men: 15 press ups
15 sit ups   20 sit ups
15 squat thrusts   20 squat thrusts

7th Kyu (yellow)

The same applies again, except for the addition of a reverse punch forward and back × 5 and a side thrust kick forward and turn × 3.
Kata – heian nidan
3-step sparring as in 8th Kyu
Exercises – Women: 7 press ups   Men: 20 press ups
20 sit ups   30 sit ups
20 squat thrusts   30 squat thrusts

6th Kyu (green)

lower block, reverse punch (f × 5); rising block, reverse punch (f × 5); outside block, reverse punch (f × 5); inside block, reverse punch (f × 5); knife-hand reverse spear finger (f × 5); turn, face punch, reverse punch × 5; front kick, reverse punch × 5; turn, side kick, reverse punch × 5; roundhouse kick × 3 forward; turn × 3 back again.
Kata – heian sandan
One-step sparring: face, stomach, front kick; block and counter with reverse punch (attack both sides of body).

Exercises – Women: 10 press ups   Men: 25 press ups
                            25 sit ups   35 sit ups
                            25 squat thrusts   35 squat thrusts

5th Kyu (purple)

lower block, ridge hand × 5
turn, rising block, rising elbow × 5
outside block, side elbow × 5
inside block, jab, reverse punch × 5
knife hand block, lower block, reverse punch × 5
face punch, stomach punch both hands × 5
front kick, double punch × 5
side kick, double punch × 5
(after each combination turn before coming back down dojo)
Kata – heian yondan
One-step sparring both sides of body: face, stomach, front kick, side kick; any block and counter.
Exercises – Women: 15 press ups   Men: 30 press ups
                            30 sit ups   40 sit ups
                            30 squat thrusts   40 squat thrusts

4th Kyu (purple and white)

Same as 5th Kyu with:

(a) roundhouse kick, reverse punch × 5, turn, same again (b) jab, reverse punch, grab head, knee strike × 5, turn – back kick × 5
Kata – heian godan
One-step sparring: both sides of body: face, stomach, front kick, side kick, roundhouse kick; any block and counter.
Exercises – Women: 15 press ups   Men: 35 press ups
                            35 sit ups   45 sit ups
                            35 squat thrusts   40 squat thrusts

3rd Kyu (brown)

           1.   lower block, ridge hand, knife hand strike × 5
turn   2.   rising block, back fist, reverse punch × 5
turn   3.   inside block, jab, reverse punch × 5
turn   4.   inside block, roundhouse, elbow strike × 5
turn   5.   jab, double punch × 5
turn   6.   jab, reverse punch, knee strike × 5
turn   7.   knife hand block, lower block, reverse punch, roundhouse kick × 5
turn   8.   front leg snap kick, back leg front kick, double punch × 5
turn   9.   front leg roundhouse kick, back leg roundhouse kick, back fist, reverse punch × 5
turn 10.   back kick × 5
turn 11.   back kick × 5
Kata – tekki shodan plus one heian kata of examiner's choice.
One-step sparring both sides of body: face, stomach, front kick, side kick, roundhouse kick and back kick; any block and counter. Two free sparring sessions lasting approximately one minute.
Exercises – Women: 20 press ups   Men: 40 press ups
                            40 sit ups   50 sit ups
                            30 squat thrusts   40 squat thrusts

2nd Kyu (brown)
Same as 3rd Kyu with one extra combination of techniques:

(a) front kick, double punch, back lower block, reverse punch forward, roundhouse kick, back-fist lunge punch.
Kata – bassai dai plus one heian kata of examiner's choice.
One-step sparring as for 3rd Kyu, 3 free style bouts lasting 1 minute.
Exercises – Women: 25 press ups   Men: 45 press ups
                        40 sit ups   50 sit ups
                        40 squat thrusts   50 squat thrusts

1st Kyu (brown and white)
Same as 2nd Kyu with one further combination:

(a) backfist, front leg side kick, reverse punch, roundhouse kick, back kick, reverse punch.
Kata – bassai dai, plus any two heian kata of examiner's choice.
Semi-free sparring plus 3 bouts freestyle, lasting approximately 1 minute.
Exercises – Women: 25 press ups   Men: 50 press ups
                        40 sit ups   50 sit ups
                        40 squat thrusts   50 squat thrusts

Shodan (black)
1. Gedan barai, ren-tsuki chudan × 3 (forward and reverse)
2. Uchi-uke, gyaku-tsuki, uraken jodan × 3 (forward and reverse)
3. Age-uke, sanbon-tsuki × 3 (forward and reverse)
4. Shuto-uke (kokutsu-dachi), gyaku-tsuki, nukite (zenkutsu-dachi) × 3 (forward and reverse)
5. Gedan-barai, age empi, yoko empi (stance change) × 3 (forward and reverse)
6. Kizami-tsuki, nagashi-uke, gyaku-tsuki, uraken, gyaku-tsuki (left and right leg × 3)
7. Mae-geri (ren-geri) jodan and chudan × 2 (that is, 4 kicks in all)
8. Mawashi-geri (ren-geri) jodan and chudan × 2 (that is, 4 kicks in all)
9. Yoko-geri-keage, yoko-geri-kekomi in kibadachi × 2 (that is, 4 kicks in all)
10. Yoko-geri-kekomi, ushiro-geri in kibadachi × 2 (that is, 4 kicks in all)
11. Mae-geri, yoko-geri-kekomi, mawashi-geri, ushiro-geri forward and turn on one leg, mae-geri, yoko-geri, ushiro-geri × 3 (change legs and repeat)
Combination
From yoi– gedan-barai, step forward mae-geri, kizami-tsuki, gyaku-tsuki, step back uchi-uke, gyaku-tsuki, step forward mawashi-geri, uraken, oi-tsuki × 2
Kata
Bassai dai and any two heian katas of the examiner's choice

Jiyu ippon kumite (left and right side of body)
1. Jodan-tsuki
2. Chudan-tsuki
3. Mae-geri
4. Jodan mawashi-geri
5. Combination attack – oi-tsuki jodan, mae-geri chudan
6. Combination attack – ren-tsuki jodan, chudan – mawashi-geri jodan

Jiyu kumite
3 × 2-minute bouts

INDEX